THE REMOTE PROJECT MANAGER

Gren Gale

A catalogue record for this book is recorded in the British Library.

ISBN 9781099908071

First published in 2019

OTHER BOOKS BY GREN GALE

Project Management for SMEs

Project Management for SMBs (US version)

Remote Work The New Normal

Dedication

There's only one person I could dedicate this book to. Always encouraging, totally supportive, the love of my life....you know who you are!

With many thanks to everyone who set about the laboured task of trying to make sense of my inane scribblings and improve what I'd written – let's hope it worked.

CONTENTS

1. Introduction

2. How to build successful remote teams

3. Technology

4. Security

5. Legal factors

6. Conclusion

1

INTRODUCTION

Why do you need this book?

Remote project management is increasingly going to be the way that projects are managed in the future. This book aims to provide you with the skills to prosper in this new paradigm

The times when a project team were all located together in the same office are fast disappearing and increasingly project managers are being asked to organise disparate groups in many different locations across the world. Language and cultural differences as well as limitations with technology and communications make each assignment a unique challenge.

This can result in a host of new demands on project managers that barely existed as little as ten years ago.....as if the job wasn't difficult enough already!!

While home working and remote working aren't necessarily the same thing, surveys indicate that the incidence of home working is increasing exponentially. A 2016 study conducted by Vodafone involving 8,000 global employees and employers[1] found that three-quarters

75%
Of companies worldwide indicated they had introduced flexible working policies

83%
Indicated a boost in productivity

61%
Stated they had increased profits as a result

Source Vodafone 'Flexible: friend or foe?' 2016

of companies worldwide had already switched to more flexible working practices. 61% believe that it had increased the company's profits and 83% reported a boost in productivity.

The COVID-19 pandemic in 2020 supercharged the move to remote working where employers faced with national and local lockdowns, multiple waves of infection and social distancing restrictions were left with a choice of remote work or no work.

Clearly not having to pay for office rents and heating and lighting is a big bonus for companies. In 2016, Dell announced plans to further expand its telecommuting and remote work initiatives, citing $12 million in annual savings from reduced office space cost[2].

Companies can tap into a pool of highly skilled resource worldwide

Faster and cheaper internet access and the exponential growth of the cloud is making the world ever smaller. Companies who need to source scarce skills that they can't find locally are now finding that they can easily tap into a much larger pool of highly skilled resource world-wide. The world's most valuable resource is knowledge and the market for services and skills is becoming truly global. In a crowded world, limiting migration is being seen as a political priority for a growing number of governments and in this environment the trend towards employing off-shore expertise is only likely to grow.

Many of the approaches that the best project managers use are far more difficult to deploy in an environment where often they're a disembodied voice in a conference call. Eye contact, body language and the feedback you gain from being in close proximity is lost. More than that, chasing people down for a brief discussion gets trickier. Informality becomes more difficult to achieve and it gets a whole lot harder to pick up on the mood of both individuals and the wider organisation. This is an environment that amplifies the potential for misunderstandings and mistrust. The term 'remote' is true on so many levels.

The absence of the face-to-face element also restricts the ability to build personal relationships. Things can get very stilted and it's far more difficult to get to know someone just from chats on audio calls. Getting to know you better over a beer as commonly happens in Europe and the US or over coffee and cakes as is popular in the Middle East isn't going to happen.

Language and accents can be problematic particularly where the quality of the audio link is poor. Cultural issues, especially with the lack of non-verbal feedback are a minefield where slights can be made without realising it no matter how polite and careful you are. On top of that working with people in different time zones can play havoc with family and social life as the division between work and leisure time becomes ever more fuzzy.

Remote project management is already with us and is growing rapidly. It's increasingly going to be the way that project management functions in the future. This book aims to provide you with the skills to prosper in this new paradigm.

It's about more than just technology

The technology is easy to acquire but the skills to choose the right tools and then use them to bind together a happy and effective team are a lot harder to find

There are a number of pieces of key technology that make distributed projects work. The team needs to be able to communicate which means as a minimum videoconferencing, instant messaging and e-mail. They'll need to share documents in a joint file repository and produce, share and track plans using a project management package.

It has become relatively easy and cheap to implement videoconferencing, so there is a tendency to just do it without considering that there might be costs to not doing it well. Good communication tools are a major asset in making remote management work.

Sharing documents and sending messages and e-mails is the sort of thing that is done as a matter of course by in-house teams but it's not unusual to experience complications with competing and potentially conflicting software in a more disparate environment. Instant messaging is handy, but not if three different messaging applications are plastering your screen and your mobile with messages. Good old e-mail is the legacy technology in all of this and has a lot of life left in it yet, but e-mails need to be used properly. All of these tools can lead to overload for individuals who are likely to receive multiples of the volumes of written communications that they would expect to see in an in-house environment.

There are literally hundreds of project management and collaboration packages. It's a complex and crowded marketplace with a variety of different offerings aimed at different audiences and market sectors. For a distributed team this is a key piece of software to get right.

Remote project management is easy to do, but very hard to do well. While the technology is easy to acquire, the skills to choose the right tools and then use them to bind together a happy and effective team are a lot harder to find. This book aims to fix this.

2

HOW TO BUILD SUCCESSFUL REMOTE TEAMS

Communication

How well you communicate and encourage the whole team to do the same will be a huge influence on the success of your project

Let's face it, remote project management is mainly about communication. If you can't get that right, you won't get anything right. Teams of any sort regardless of their location work a whole lot better if they know what's expected of them, understand what the whole project is trying to achieve and are kept up to date on progress. This is a challenge for an office based team but a much bigger test for a remote team. How well you communicate and encourage the whole team to do the same will be a huge influence on the success of your project.

In this section we're not going to talk about communications technology. There's plenty about that later in the book, but we are going to talk about how you communicate and what you need to consider in that.

So what's so different when you're remote?

So you may be asking, what's so different about communication in remote teams? You might feel you're a pretty good communicator and just because you're in front of a camera with a headset on why would that be about to change? That's exactly what I thought when I started managing my first remote project. By the end I'd totally changed my view.

Managing a geographically distributed team is full of challenges that don't present themselves in local teams. These vary from poor technology, lack of non-verbal feedback, inability to have a quick chat to resolve things, to cultural differences, language and accent.

Project managers have lots of time and schedule pressures on them so it's easy to plough on under pressure and ignore all of the new challenges introduced by working remotely.

So let's consider the simple stuff about communication.

Non-verbal communication

Communication consists of far more than the words that come out of your mouth. When you speak you move your hands, body, eyes and head continuously. All of these movements are closely coordinated with your speech and form the total communication[3].

Body language has been around for as long as Homo Sapiens and spoken words for between 50 and 100 thousand years, so we've had plenty of practice at both working in harmony. After Alexander Graham Bell patented the first telephone in 1876 we've barely had 150 years to adapt to using words without body language, so it's hardly surprising that we're not very good at it.

Ray L Birdwhistell an American anthropologist estimated from his research that 65 percent of communication is done non-verbally and more astonishingly that we can make and recognise around 250,000 facial expressions. Barbara and Allan Pease in The Definitive Book of Body Language[15] further estimated that body language is responsible for between 60 and 80 percent of the impact made in negotiations and that people form 60 to 80 percent of their first impression about a new person in less than four minutes.

Research by psychologists at Harvard University also showed how women are far better readers of body language than men. The researchers showed short films of a man and woman communicating with the soundtracks removed and asked the subjects to work out what they were talking about. The women read the situation correctly 87 percent of the time, while the men scored only 42 percent.

All of these non-verbal clues are lost in a voice-only meeting and many are lost or are considerably depreciated in a videoconference. This represents a huge loss in the richness and effectiveness of communication. As a result the potential for misunderstandings or misinterpretations is huge.

You need to be fully aware of the implications of separating the verbal and non-verbal parts of your communication. They won't be obvious to you of course, you'll still be pulling the usual expressions and doing the subtle stuff your face and body does when you communicate face-to-face but no-one else will be seeing it.

Non-verbal communication can consist of:

- Facial expressions

- Gaze and eye contact

- Eye expression - pupil dilation, blink rate, direction of gaze, degree of opening of the eyes and facial expression specifically in the eye area

- Gestures

- Posture

- Touch and smell

- Appearance

All of these convey a huge amount of information in addition to speech.

Facial expressions transmit emotion and social signals. Argyle and Ingram in 1972 showed that when we communicate we look at each other frequently. We tend to make eye contact more when we're listening than talking (Exline and Winters 1965) and other studies have shown we make more eye contact with people we like and that eye contact is related to power. High power individuals maintain high levels of eye contact while both talking and listening (Ellyson, Dovido and Fehr 1981). There is of course no eye contact in an audioconference and our natural eye contact routine becomes distorted in a videoconference.

Important information like approval and disapproval, happiness and anger or even surprise can be misjudged or lost without these non-verbal clues.

You must have found that you can get on with some people instantly whereas others seem much harder. This is often because of the subtle workings of body language than what is actually being spoken. One study by Argle, Salter, Nicholson, Williams and Burgess in 1970 showed that non-verbal communication had five times as much influence on inter-personal relationships than did verbal.

Gestures of course can also transmit a lot of information and this varies from country to country. For instance Italians have a tradition of making use of hand and arm movements[4] in expressing themselves whereas the English tend to be more reserved. Voice itself can lead to assumptions about culture, social class, competence and personality type.

As a result you are likely to find it more difficult to work out how you're being viewed by people you interact with remotely, particularly over audio-only links. I've certainly found this.

Knowing when to speak on an audio-only call is also more difficult. When someone is speaking their body language gives off clues that say they don't want to be interrupted. The person interrupting also tends to provide a thank you or sorry in their body language when they interrupt. I worked on a project where I attended regular meetings led by a senior manager who had a habit of pausing in thought, mid-sentence before continuing to talk. The people in the room were getting body language signals that he was going to continue. I was on an audio-only link and found it very difficult to know when to break in.

People also use body language to show they'd like to interrupt. Arms waving, body leaning forwards or head nodding as well as facial and eye expression can all indicate that you want to break into the conversation.

Research by Rutter and Stephenson in 1977 indicated the impact of this lack of non-verbal clues. It showed that there are fewer interruptions in audio conferences than when people meet face-to-face. Adding to this is that conversation on a video call isn't truly duplex. When one person talks everyone else has to shut up and wait their turn which makes communication very stilted. Because of the way the internet works where everything transmitted is first split up into packets, there is an almost unavoidable delay in video calls as everything is chopped up and then reassembled in real time also making interruption a little more fraught.

Non-verbal communication is also highly connected to culture with some gestures having often wildly varying meanings in different cultures. For example while good eye contact is praised and usual in the US and Europe, it can be seen as a sign of disrespect and challenge in other cultures, including Asian and African [11].

In some situations the lack of body language can work to your advantage. For instance, if you feel you have a very good case, it may be better to negotiate in audio-only because research shows that the person with the best case tends to win in audio-only negotiations. Face-to-face people have more of a tendency to be influenced by wanting the non-verbal feedback of approval and this can influence who wins the argument[5].

There are ways that you can try to compensate for a lack of non-verbal communication. Keep reading, we'll be covering this.

Communication styles

There are a variety of communication styles. Everyone is a little different and there are vast swathes of literature written about this. We're not going to cover well-trodden ground but do want to emphasise that being an entirely remote presence tends to exaggerate your existing style, particularly where voice-only is available and no live video.

You need to be aware of this and it may require reflecting on your communication style. You will find with some thought and effort you can use words, phrasing and tone to counter this and communicate more effectively.

Think about how you're getting information over. Be clear and ask questions if you have any suspicion that you've been misunderstood. Avoid aggression no matter how wound up you might feel. Keep it calm and polite and have a good scream in private once the meeting is over. Politeness not only keeps people happy but it's also more likely to achieve the desired results. Aggression is never a good idea in project management but for a remote project manager I'd go as far as saying it's a disaster. It's that much easier to turn people off and that much harder to repair the relationship after an outburst. You need these people to deliver your project so don't alienate them!

Without going over the top, try to behave in a way that is rewarding to the people you're interfacing with and try to take care of their self-esteem by praising effort and success. I'd advise this for any project manager in any situation but it's particularly good practice when you're not in close proximity and your connection with your team is a little more tenuous.

Working remotely means in many cases you can't meet all of the people you're regularly interfacing with, but if it's feasible to meet any of them then I'd strongly recommend you do this and as early in the project as possible. It adds a personal closeness that is hard to generate in any other way. We just seem to be able to communicate and get on better with people if we've had at least one face-to-face meeting with them. It seems to leave an imprint of intimacy that never goes away.

Active Listening

Being able to listen and absorb what you hear is an important skill in both our business and personal lives. Everyone seems to like a good listener and to complain about the person who likes the sound of their own voice. When you're working remotely, listening skills become especially important given the lack of non-verbal communication.

Research suggests that we only absorb between 25 and 50 percent of what we hear and given the greater opportunity for distraction, being remote is likely to reduce that further. To counter this, you might want to try to practice 'Active Listening'. Active Listening is used widely in the counselling community. It involves making a conscious effort to not only hear the words being communicated but the complete message.

This means paying careful attention to what is being communicated and not becoming distracted or bored. It's so easy to become distracted when you're in front of a computer on a conference call.

There are e-mails and messages popping up in front of you, that report you have to finish by the end of the day and even a sports result to follow! There's nothing more embarrassing than becoming diverted in the middle of a call, only to be asked what you think about something that's being discussed and nothing more irritating to be on a call and hearing the clicking of a mouse and keyboard coming from one or more participant.

While someone is talking try to let them know that you're listening, avoid any distracting thoughts, ask them to clarify anything you're not sure about and summarise what they've said from time to time. Try not to come to judgements too quickly and to not interrupt them with counter arguments until you've absorbed what they're trying to convey.

Clearly if you were counselling someone, becoming bored or distracted would be unforgivable and there's no way you would gain the confidence of your client. The same very much applies to remote management. Your job is to engender confidence, you need to listen, understand and remember what is being said.

Nonviolent Communication (NVC)

Unresolved conflict destroys teams – conflict in a distributed team can be particularly toxic. Rivalries, vendettas and disagreements can fester much more readily in a remote environment, so it's important to do everything that you can to try to avoid this. Nonviolent communication is a way of removing the negative and adversarial elements from conversation to achieve a better result.

In the remote project manager role it's very easy to fall into negative feelings about the people you're interfacing with and managing and to find yourself in adversarial situations. These aren't always easy to resolve face to face but have the potential to be quite corrosive when you're remote. The way you are viewed by people you've never met in person will largely be judged from what you say and how you express yourself. Being viewed as argumentative and judgemental isn't good. Being viewed as listening, calm and empathetic is likely to be regarded a lot more positively.

NVC has been used as a very effective resource for mediation in resolving conflicts and has been utilised in Rwanda, Sierra Leone, Bosnia and Croatia. Your project is unlikely to experience quite that level of conflict but NVC has proved to be very effective where people from differing cultures are trying to resolve disputes and disagreements.

Often our judgements get in the way of understanding what is happening. NVC teaches us to observe without evaluating, for example saying 'You're so obstructive' makes an evaluation of behaviour but doesn't actually tell us why you've made that evaluation. Replacing this with 'I've noticed that you disagree with a lot of my proposals' is better given it's factual and non-judgemental.

NVC was created by Marshall B Rosenberg [6] and explains that NVC is a process for more successful and empathetic communication and that there are four components to this process:

1. Observations

2. Feelings

3. Needs

4. Requests

Observation, as we've noted above is keeping judgement and criticism out of it and trying to discern and then communicate the facts.

It's natural to react to a critical, adversarial or accusatory statement with a defensive statement or counter attack. We tend to take these attacking statements personally and once the conversation starts moving down this track it has a habit of escalating to an unhappy conclusion. Rosenberg describes this as 'life-alienating conversation'. Other examples of life-alienating conversation are denial of responsibility, comparisons with others and the assertion that some people are simply 'bad' or evil'.

So having observed in a non-judgemental manner, the next step is to express your feelings. Identifying your emotions and being brave enough to express them helps you connect more effectively with others. So in our example after pointing out that they disagree with lots of your proposals, you might say 'and that makes me feel annoyed and frustrated'. NVC also instructs that you should take responsibility for your feelings, in other words explain why you feel that way. So we might say 'and that makes me feel annoyed and frustrated because it slows everything down and I'm feeling anxious that I won't be able deliver the project on time'. There is more than a subtle difference in this. The first statement solely blames the other party for making me annoyed and frustrated, the second recognises my thinking behind the feelings of annoyance and frustration and in particular states my needs (to deliver the project on time). Needs are the acknowledgement of the stimulus for our feelings.

So now we've managed to address what we've observed, how we're feeling and what our needs are without criticising, accusing, aggression or blaming. The next stage is to express what we would like to happen to make things good for us all - our 'request'.

This is a specific request for action that will fulfil our needs. It's important that this is a positive request, not a negative one. So 'stop disagreeing or the project won't deliver in time' won't do. Our request needs to be genuinely a request and not a demand and should not imply blame. It might be a series of requests and it must be specific not vague or ambiguous or it may be impossible or very difficult to fulfil. So in our example, you could say 'would it be possible to schedule a short weekly meeting for us both to discuss my proposals at an early stage to get us both on the same sheet?'

So in summary, when someone communicates negatively, we can blame ourselves, blame others or alternatively sense the feelings and needs hidden in the other person's negative message. If we respond negatively we're unlikely to make much progress. The more we can express our feelings and needs the easier it is for the others to respond positively and with empathy.

So you may be thinking this all sounds a bit touchy feely and if you do think that, you'd be right. It's also quite difficult to do and if you're serious about trying this you should probably invest some time and money in training. However this is a widely used technique that has been proven to deliver excellent results in a wide variety of situations.

In a remote management scenario being able to avoid conflict, listen and generate empathy is far more likely to produce results than some misguided macho project management approach. So if you're working as a remote project manager I'd strongly recommend that you familiarise yourself with NVC.

For more information on NVC please read Marshall B. Rosenberg's excellent book Nonviolent Communication - A Language for Life.

Open or closed questions

Open questions are ones that ask the respondent to think and reflect. They are unlikely ever to result in a one word answer. Closed questions are ones that can be answered with a single word or phrase often just yes or no. An example of a closed question would be 'You have finished it, haven't you' whereas an open question might go 'Can you give me a bit more detail on how the task is going?'

In some instances you do need a simple yes or no answer and closed questions are appropriate. However in a scenario where you're trying to encourage teamwork, working with a much lower level of feedback and running a much higher risk of misunderstandings, it's better to let people speak rather than cutting them off with closed questions.

Humour

I like to build a bit of humour into the way I work. I often find the best way to diffuse a tricky situation is with a little humour, and well if you can't enjoy your work then life gets pretty dull. However while this is very effective face-to-face, from my experience I'm not convinced that this is the best approach for remote project management. A flippant comment in one culture (or even the same culture) may at best fall flat and at worst offend someone and if you're unable to see their reaction and them to see your smiling face then I think you're playing with fire.

It's all about building confidence and the people who hear your disembodied voice or read your e-mails need to feel they have total faith in you. So by all means stay light but at all times business-like unless you feel you know the person you're talking to really well.

Written communication

Written communication comes in various forms during a project, including e-mails, instant messages, project reports and documents describing the project. In many projects there are tons of the stuff!

The main thing with all written communication is to bear in mind the people you're writing to. Your first language may not be theirs so keep the wording simple and straightforward.

You might want to think about how you present progress to both your management and your team. An informed team is more likely to be a happy one. For a large dispersed team, you might want to consider producing a newsletter especially if you can encourage all parts of the team to contribute. I ran an 18 month IT project with teams in India, US, Australia and England. Some of the work was also subcontracted to third party organisations. This meant we had a large team spread across four continents. Making all of those guys feel like a single team was always going to be a challenge and one thing we did was to publish a newsletter. Hard work to bring it all together but it was well received and hopefully it made a difference.

Formal reporting needs to be carried out and if you're using a decent project management package this should allow you to produce reports quickly to a format agreed with your management. Formal reporting can become a time consuming bugbear where there is no automation.

Key communication recommendations

- Don't assume communicating with a remote team works the same was as with a local one.
- Lack of non-verbal feedback, cultural, language, accent and technology issues will make it harder to communicate effectively.
- Be clear and ask questions if you have any suspicion that you've been misunderstood.
- Avoid using aggressive language and tone - it's harder to repair a remote relationship after an outburst.
- If it's feasible, try to meet as many of your team members as possible face-to-face at least once
- Use Active Listening – make sure you listen, understand and remember what is being said.
- Study Nonviolent Communication as an effective means of both avoiding and resolving disputes.
- Be careful with humour – it may at best fall flat and at worst offend someone.

Respecting different cultures

While you might feel more at home with people from your own cultural background, the research seems to show that teams profit from their diversity

Managing a remote team increasingly is moving away from an office based team split into home and office workers into truly global teams. I've worked in a team who were spread across North, South and Central America, Europe, Asia and Australasia. Many big companies have offices in several countries and even small ones are becoming increasingly more distributed.

In an ever more global business community, project teams can be assembled from talent pools located all over the world so it's important to understand the issues as well as the advantages that managing such diverse teams can bring.

We often take for granted the way we communicate with one another. So many aspects of the way we interact with people, address issues and make decisions are based on our cultural upbringing. In a multicultural team how everyone communicates is critical and can be the difference between a successful team and one that finds it has more differences than things in common.

Positives

While you might feel more at home with people from your own cultural background, the research seems to show that teams profit from their diversity. It makes sense that a team with a greater diversity of ages, skills and backgrounds is likely to bring more to the party than one consisting of people who all have a similar outlook on life. Scott E. Page, professor and director of the Center of the Study of Complex Systems at the University of Michigan has demonstrated that more diverse groups outperform like-minded experts[7]. Concluding that 'progress depends as much on our collective differences as it does on our individual IQ scores.'

Enterprises large and small can gain positive advantage from developing intercultural expertise. Not only does this help them run more effective and innovative teams but it also empowers them to interact in a more self-assured way with suppliers, customers and prospective customers wherever they're located in the world.

Five rules

While it may sound a little trite to boil down how you work with people from different cultures into five rules, I'm going to do it anyway.

1. Recognise the existence of different cultures in your organisation and act on this

2. Be open minded, respectful and tolerant

3. Understand and acknowledge any difficulties in communicating

4. Address language difficulties directly

5. Consider developing a rule book.

Recognise the existence of different cultures

The single biggest mistake you can make is to assume that everyone you work with worldwide is going to respond well to your usual style. To do this is to run the risk of alienating any members of your team not from your culture.

There is huge variety in the way people communication worldwide with many cultures for example putting a higher emphasis on non-verbal communication. Western European and English speaking cultures tend to place a stronger emphasis on verbal communication whereas Asian, African, Arab, East European and Latin American cultures have a tendency to make more use of non-verbal cues. Claire B. Halverson in her book Cultural Context Inventory[12] describes the former as Low Context Cultures and the latter as High Context where non-verbal factors such as voice tone, gestures, facial expression and eye movement are far more significant. Especially in situations where you may not be able to see these non-verbal clues, it's very important that you listen carefully and ask questions to clarify.

It's very easy for difference to lead to stereotyping, misunderstanding and blame which makes it important to recognise this and replace conflict with empathy and understanding. If you're working with a diverse team then take the time to research the basic dos and don'ts for other cultures. Also bear in mind that it's rarely as simple as deciding how you should treat someone based only on their cultural background and from what region of the world they originate. People from the same country can find lots of differences and similarities in for example gender, race, education, religion, cultural upbringing, social class and social outlook. They may also find that the things they have in common such as a love of sport, music or movies transcends all of their differences and cements a bond. I've met a number of Indian nationals in my working life and although we haven't always had that much in common, once we start discussing

34

cricket all of the differences fall away and we're suddenly talking a common language. Effective Multicultural Teams by Claire Halverson and Aqeel Tirmizi[13] as the title suggests is a specialist study of this and is an excellent read.

A few years ago I ran a project in London for a Japanese company. Taking the trouble to read a book on Japanese culture was not only a fascinating insight into a different culture but also paid dividends for the project and in particular helped us to successfully negotiate with our client in the knowledge that the Japanese approach to negotiation differed significantly to that used in Western Europe. Research does pay off!

Even the simplest communication can be misunderstood, for instance 'Yes' can be a dangerous word. In some cultures it means 'I agree' in others 'I heard what you just said'. There's a world of difference between those two and the wrong understanding could be disastrous. 'No' can be just as tricky. In some cultures including my own, people avoid saying no out of politeness. It seems very direct to say no, so they try to soften it by phrases such as 'I don't think it's right for us at this time' or 'I'm not sure that will work but we'll think about it' and then hope the topic never resurfaces. Non-verbal assent and disagreement can also be misleading. If you see a nodding head on a video link in response to a question, you might assume that means 'yes' but in some parts of Greece, Serbia, Bulgaria and Turkey, a nodding head means 'no'[11].

In some cultures there is a strong desire to please authority figures so people find 'no' hard to say. I was delivering a back office IT system for a company in England a while back. We were using a software company in India to deliver the system. As we approached our first delivery I kept asking them if they were on track and was constantly given reassurance that everything was going well. With our User Testing systems and team all ready to go, we received a call early in the morning on delivery day saying they'd be three weeks late.

They'd been so desperate to tell us what we wanted that they had literally worked day and night to deliver and finally gave up early in the morning on the day it was due for delivery. Ten out of ten for effort, but zero out of ten for trust. With a greater appreciation of the Indian culture at that time, we would almost certainly have seen a better outcome.

Be open minded, respectful and tolerant

What might seem fine in your culture might be seen as odd or rude in another. There are lots of examples of this from blowing your nose in public to a variety of hand signals (we won't go into that!), toilet habits, and even the way you laugh.

Customs and habits differ from one culture to another. Some people habitually talk at a high or low volume. Some may be more direct or more reserved in showing emotion. Employees in some cultures have a need to exhibit a high degree of presenteeism or at least not leave the office before their boss does. Some are keen to display a high work ethic and others appear more laid back. There are all sorts of assumptions that you might make about these behaviours based on your own cultural background which may turn out to be well wide of the mark. So you need to be open minded and respectful. We tend to lack awareness of our own biases and it's easy to place stereotype and cultural assumptions on others. Just because it seems a bit strange to you doesn't mean it's viewed the same way in another culture.

You also need to be aware of hierarchies. How senior are the people you're interfacing with? What are their expectations of how you'll interact with them according to their business and social hierarchy norms?

Attitudes to gender and age differ around the world. In your culture men and women may communicate equally with each other, but you may have to interact with people from a tradition where men have a more dominant role. In many cultures age has an exaggerated importance and deference is to the oldest person in the room. This may result in resistance to a younger person taking the lead. What you can do is to make sure you introduce yourself fully so people understand who you are and where you fit in.

In some environments senior managers are addressed as 'sir' in others this would be anathema both to the person addressing them and the senior manager.

None of these issues are insuperable, but it's important you understand them and work with not against them.

In a pressured delivery environment it's easy either deliberately or out of ignorance to impose what you see as normal on everyone else because you think that's the best way of reaching the finishing line.

Understand and acknowledge any difficulties in communicating

If you were unable to understand someone or think that they didn't understand you then it's important to say something about it. Avoid being rude or offensive, but patiently explain what the issue or misunderstanding is. It's nearly always better to be open than to let a problem in communication go unaddressed and potentially lead to bigger issues later.

The main thing is to be polite, so if you think you didn't understand what someone meant, try saying something like: "I'm not sure I understood you. Could we go over that again?" Alternatively, if you think that someone did not understand you, try something like: "Let's review things to make sure we've all understood."

Social routines

There are some social routines that are universal in every culture. In normal conversation these rely heavily on non-verbal feedback. Is someone upset with you, do they feel unappreciated or are they fed up with you interrupting constantly or seemingly being unable to listen? They may tell you these things straight but more likely in face-to-face communication it will be written all over their expression and body language. You may not be able to see either as a remote manager, so err on the side of safety. If you think you've caused upset, better to over-compensate than just charge on.

Thank people for work they've done. Whatever people interpret from your other actions and dialogue, it's impossible to mistake a thank you. Saying thank you is important in teams of any composition but really makes the difference in a culturally and geographically disparate team. Building team spirit is so important and saying thank you is big part of that.

Don't be afraid to apologise. You will make mistakes, you will make gaffes and you may well upset people. Make it very clear that you're apologising. In a remote team it's easy to think the moment has gone when you're mulling over something you said in a meeting. If you think you made a gaffe or upset someone then it's worth following it up with an instant message, e-mail or call after the meeting. I have one particularly embarrassing incident in mind where I'd managed to twice exclude a senior manager from an e-mail circulation list after they had complained about this the first time. This manager was in another country where deference to your manager was a very strong cultural norm. I made an apology in a meeting but thinking it over afterwards, it hadn't been sufficient. I should have written at that point to further apologise. I didn't and relations between us were never quite the same after that. I really had lost the moment. Don't do the same.

Listen and don't interrupt too much. It's a poor manager who interrupts and doesn't listen, but you'll find that amplified if you're a voice on a conference call from the other side of the world. Being listened to and not interrupted equates to being valued.

Language

In a project team located all over the world, language and accents can be a real problem. The best advice is to make sure you ask if you don't understand anything, but you may need to go a step further.

As described in Chapter 3 – Technology, more vendors of messaging and videoconferencing software are offering translation options and this is likely to be an area that improves rapidly with Artificial Intelligence starting to move into the sphere of translation. This is unlikely ever to be perfect and you may still need to ask questions but translation will improve everyone's understanding of what's going on. If you are having issues and you don't have translation software then you may need to include a translator in the meeting.

If you are in a role that regularly interfaces with teams who speak a different language to yours then consider learning that language. Being bilingual will also improve your employability and in all probability pay rate! Speaking two of English, Spanish, French and Mandarin Chinese with around 3 billion speakers won't hurt your career prospects.

A combination of poor quality sound and differing accents can be a real issue and one that starts to lead to embarrassment if you have to keep asking for clarifications. Again an area where you have to tread carefully and give reasons why you're asking for so many clarifications rather than an implied 'you're not speaking clearly'. I worked on a project where a large team from all over Europe and Asia met weekly to discuss progress. One team in the Far East spoke in what to my ears was heavily accented English over a very bad line. We managed, but at times my frequent requests for repetition felt embarrassing to me.

One way of combatting the difficulty of understanding accented speech is to practise. This may sound sort of obvious but it's backed up by research and it's something that's missed by most people. The research shows that native language listeners often have difficulty understanding non-native accented speakers and that the emphasis on making the communication successful is usually placed on the non-native speaker, with frequent requests for repetition or clarity[8]. So if for instance you you're a native English speaker and have a meeting with a non-native English speaking Brazilian once a week, then go to YouTube and search for 'Brazilians speaking English' and you'll find lots of practice material.

Avoid colloquialisms. It's so tempting to use the colloquialisms that you use in everyday speaking but this isn't a good idea. Keep your language simple, there is so much opportunity for misunderstandings. When the English talk about window shopping, they're unlikely to be talking about starting work on restoring a house and if the French say 'On va lécher les vitrines' they probably won't be out to see what the local windows taste like and yet both of these expressions mean exactly the same thing!

Avoid slang and profanity. Using slang or obscene language can make you hard to understand and may be viewed as very offensive. Slang and profanity require an in-depth understanding of a language and their meaning is highly dependent on context.

The brain has to work hard when it translates and can find even the normal use of language difficult, particularly where two words sound similar. Throwing in additional challenges is likely to lead to confusion, so the best advice is to keep well clear of foul language.

Consider developing a rule book

Consider all of the points made above and think about developing a rule book or training or both.

The tendency is to wait until something goes wrong before putting rules or training in place, but with the sort of issues raised in this section it's entirely possible that you won't discover any damage until it's too late. It's easy to get a bad reputation, difficult to lose it. Don't set yourself up for a fall through lack of thought or ignorance.

Key recommendations in respecting other cultures

- How well everyone communicates in a multicultural team can be the difference between a successful team and one that finds it has more differences than things in common
- Take the time to research the basic dos and don'ts for other cultures
- Be open minded and respectful. Just because something seems a bit strange to you doesn't mean its viewed the same way in another culture
- Keep your language simple and straightforward and avoid colloquialisms
- Avoid slang and profanity. Using slang or obscene language can make you hard to understand and may be viewed as very offensive
- Thank people for work they've done. Whatever your cultural background it's impossible to mistake a thank you
- You will make mistakes and you may well upset people. Don't be afraid to apologise
- Think about developing a rule book or training or both.

How do you manage?

You'll need to put in hard graft to allow yourself to be more organised, more flexible and more communicative

Humans aren't designed for remote communication

So how do you manage remotely? If you carry on doing what you've always done then the answer is likely to be 'very badly'. Take it from me, managing a remote team is a totally different paradigm.

Humans were designed for interaction and communication and no matter how hard you try this can never be as good in a remote scenario as it is where everyone is working in the same room. The subtle messages that people unconsciously express in face-to-face meetings are often lost in a remote meeting.

There are costs to working remotely. The single most important point you need to appreciate is that if you want this to work then you're going to have to work a lot harder than you would in a 'normal' environment. You'll need to put in hard graft to allow yourself to be more organised, more flexible and more communicative to make up for what is being lost.

As a remote manager you might find yourself trying to manage or interface with large numbers of people spread across numerous locations. The chances are you'll be working on audio-only a lot of the time. You won't be picking up those non-verbal clues we talked about earlier or be able to pop around to someone's desk to take the sting out of a situation you're worried is starting to escalate.

In fact you might not be able to have a chat with anyone at all, you might be limited to progress meetings whenever they're scheduled into people's diaries. In a recent project I worked from London with a group spread across the East and West United States. Given the different time zones and that these were busy people, the only way to arrange meetings was to have regular dates booked into diaries. Impromptu meetings were very difficult to arrange.

As an experienced project manager, I found this very frustrating. When I find issues I like to address them quickly. I could fire off e-mails but often had to wait a few days until I could have a proper discussion of the issue with a view to finding a full solution. In this situation problems tend to pile up. I would find a meeting originally called to deal with a single issue ending up trying to discuss multiple issues because new ones had arisen in the time between finding the original issue and holding the meeting.

I've also found in this arms-length environment that working out that people are becoming unhappy with you is a lot more difficult than you might think and clearly this can lead to very dangerous situations.

So how do you make it work?

You have to try to compensate for the diminished communication and a natural reticence that most people have to managing people they haven't met, often can't even see and can't hope to know that well.

As we've mentioned earlier, in an ideal world you should try to visit and meet as many of your team as is feasible as this creates a bond that helps communication and builds understanding and empathy. However this isn't always possible. Your team may be too widely distributed to ever hope to be able to meet them all. I worked on a project with team members all over the world from North and South America to East Asia and Australasia. There was never a hope of meeting them all. Time and budgets and your own personal limitations may preclude this. So there is a pressing need to compensate.

Understand who you're talking to

Top of your priority list is to get hold of the company's Organisation Chart. Every company has one, but sadly it's usually out of date. In one project for a multi-national company I found myself talking to people in several countries without having a clue as to their position in the organisation. Most senior managers warm to a bit of deference but in some cultures this deference isn't just preferred it's programmed in from birth. Act like these guys are junior members of your team and you're in for a rough ride.

So if you can't get an Organisation Chart or it's inaccurate then use LinkedIn, the company's website or just ask people. Company e-mails usually contain a signature which may give a good idea of status, notwithstanding the tendency especially in big companies for everyone to claim they're some sort of manager! If their local guys are showing them huge deference and you're treating them as an equal (or less!) then they may find this undermining and irritating which ultimately will be damaging to you.

National characteristics can be misleading. To most Americans and Europeans, many Indians sound very polite and deferential. Given the cultural norms in Europe and the US and the sort of personality that manages to climb the greasy pole, there's a natural tendency to view someone who comes across this way as being less senior. That would be a very big mistake to make. To a British ear the way that many Americans express themselves sounds brash and confident, maybe even a little intimidating, but actually they're just as full of uncertainty and insecurity as the rest of us. Don't be fooled into applying your own cultural norms to others.

Are you in charge?

If you're a remote project manager in a large organisation despite your best efforts to communicate effectively it can still difficult to know what's happening on the ground.

Stuff goes on that is very difficult for you to know about. This is hard to keep up with if you're in the same office, but virtually impossible to track if you're not. It's usually the sort of thing that comes out in water cooler gossip and spreads like wildfire around an office. It's frequently said that the smokers, huddling together and gossiping away in an often freezing outdoor smoking area are truly the only ones who know what's going on.

So try to keep on top of this by asking your team members and colleagues at meetings if there's anything new you should know about. Take it from me, you're often the last to know, with everyone assuming that you already do given it's such common knowledge on the ground.

Build credibility and respect

If you're going to prove your professional credibility you need to be very organised. Maintain risk, issue and action lists and keep your plans up to date. Share each of these with your team. Keep on top of change.

Make sure you have the facts at your fingertips. Do your homework and understand what is going on. If there are gaps in your knowledge then try very hard to fill them. If you're working in an unfamiliar technical area, carry out your own research to get up to speed. You can't afford to be just good enough, you have to look like a superstar at the end of a telephone line. I told you it was harder than working face-to-face!

The way you act and treat the people in your team will earn you respect. You need to respect their culture, customs and personalities as well as running the project in such a way as to gain respect.

Inevitably project management involves a degree of subtle manipulation to get what you want when you need it from the wide groups of people who are involved in delivering a project. More often than not you're not the line manager of most of the people involved in your project, so persistence, persuasion and a degree of subtle manipulation are all useful tools to get what you need.

But be a little careful with this. It's easy for people to take offence or see you as a political manipulator or worse still someone more interested in promoting themselves than working for the good of the organisation. The most respected people are those who appear to have no hidden agenda but are working towards the common goal.

Politics

My least favourite part of project management is the politics. It's hard to avoid and while it tends to be endemic in large organisations with rival personalities trying to get ahead of each other, I've seen it in companies of a few hundred employees where the rivalry can be even more bitter. It's never a good idea to get involved. Your job is to deliver in spite of the politics and it's often difficult to be seen as an honest broker without someone identifying you has being 'on the other side'!

Well the bad news is that as a remote project manager, as I've just said, it's that much more difficult to really know what's going on. There's no magic formula, but be really aware of politics. Go out of your way to emphasise that your job is to deliver and that you have no interest in getting involved in the politics (of course you can't actually refer to politics – no-one would actually admit to making political moves). However your remoteness can also be an asset. If you play your hand right, your very distance can make you seem above the fray.

Easy to say but difficult to do, you really have to try to be everyone's friend and no-one's enemy. Be open, be honest, be clear ....and be careful!

Build teamwork and communicate better

Project managers often don't pay sufficient attention to building teamwork in office based teams. A tight-knit team will always achieve more than a collection of individuals which is why it's vital that you give serious thought to how you're going to bind a remote team together.

No matter how good a communicator you are, you'll need to raise the bar as a remote project manager. Project managers spend a lot of their life communicating. Remote project managers need to go the extra mile. We'll describe how in the following sections.

Show your face

I've been in far too many videoconferences where everyone shuts down the video and sticks to audio. This is fine where the line bandwidth is poor or you have a huge number of participants but try to avoid it otherwise.

Don't worry about what anyone else on the call is doing, go on to video whenever possible, a real face is just that, not a disembodied voice. Even if you can't pick up their body language, let everyone else pick up yours. Hardly anyone looks good on a video link, especially wearing a headset and your reading glasses but put your vanity to one side, being seen makes you a lot more real and credible.

Buy as high quality a camera as you can afford, a clear high definition image is better than a fuzzy one. Better cameras will also cope better with low or imperfect lighting. You may have to bear the sight of your wrinkles, grey hairs or acne in a little more focus than you'd like, but don't worry about it. It's all about projecting you as a person.

One other tip if you're working from home is to minimise the distractions behind your face. You want your audience concentrating on you, not your kids playing behind you or your underwear on the clothes dryer at the back of your room. Ideally have a part of your house set up as an office. Test how the backdrop looks and have it look clean and professional. Yes, you want to show your face, but you also want to show you're as organised at home as your team will expect you to be on the project.

The power of small talk in cementing teams

You might want to think about a 'Wall of Fame'. Include a photo of yourself and each team member and a short description of their background and hobbies. It can live in a shared on-line space that everyone can get to. Prepare yours first to act as a template and encouragement for everyone else to complete theirs.

Most humans need small talk (as well as professional work talk) to interact well. In fact many historians believe that human language evolved as a way of gossiping[9]. The Wall facilitates this. It lets everyone on the team know what their colleagues look like and it provides scope for small talk – hey you're a movie buff, keen cyclist, music lover. It opens up everyone's background and interests and that helps build the feeling of being in a team. A little small talk goes a long way to building the sense of being included and part of something and that's often lacking in geographically dispersed teams.

One of the guys I worked for used to start his weekly meetings by asking each of the attendees to say (briefly!) what they had been up to over the weekend. It's tricky to do this for a big meeting but if you've a number less than seven it's worth a try – again it's about getting people to open up and know each other better.

People are notoriously bad at arriving on time for meetings. Use that waiting time to chat. Keep a cache of topics, check what's in the news, but don't get too carried away. Politics and your team's love lives are better left well alone!

Social Activities

I'm sure you're far more concerned with delivering your project than being social secretary for your team, but social activities are a good way of building teamwork and as strange as it sounds, can work well remotely. We talk about loneliness and stress later in this section. Those are emotions that can apply to any team members and particularly to someone new joining the team. Involving new joiners in social activities is a good way of breaking the ice and it's often easier to persuade someone to attend a remote activity than it is a face-to-face one. Unless you're desperate to do this yourself, you may want to appoint a project social organiser. This is one job that there never seems to be a shortage of volunteers for.

Here are some ideas for remote social activities:-

- A quiz night is always a good ice breaker and if your organisation is big enough then you can break into teams. A number of videoconferencing tools facilitate break-out groups making this easy to do. Buy a few drinks and it becomes a pub quiz! You can either research and set the questions yourself or use sites like TriviaMaker and TriviaBliss to produce the questions for you.

- Charades works well over a video link. Come up with an idea, say whether it's a book, film, TV show, play, person or something from another category and then act it out starting by saying how many syllables you're acting out.

- Movie night. Vote on what movie you all want to watch and share a Netflix, YouTube or Amazon Prime screen. There are a whole host of apps and browser add-ons specifically designed for this, try TwoSeven, Netflix Party and Watch2Gether. They'll allow you to synchronise watching videos with your friends together with a chat window so you can all make comments about the movie while it's running.

- Smartphone Apps. If you like word games you might want to give WordswithFriends or Scrabble Go a try. They're both Android and iOS word game apps. You can have a videoconference running at the same time as you're playing the game on your phones.

- Pictionary. If your videoconferencing package supports whiteboards then it's easy to play Pictionary but even if it doesn't pen and paper in front of the camera works just as well. You can use Pictionary Random Word Generator to come up with words.

- Two truths, one lie. Really great icebreaker. Each person on the video call tells two true things about themselves and one lie. Everyone else has to guess which is which.

- Murder Mystery Party. Why not set up a murder mystery party. Try The Murder Mystery Store or My Mystery Party, both sell virtual games relatively cheaply.

- Donut is an extension to Slack, a popular workplace messaging tool. It pairs people randomly together in your company for a 30 minute chat as a way of getting to know people. Messaging is less pressured but you might want to do this face-to-face on a videoconference instead.

- Plant growing competitions. This works a treat. The idea is that each participant (you might want to make it teams) buys a packet of seeds of exactly the same plant. Everyone then plants, tends and grows. Pick something like chillies, cucumbers or tomatoes that produce a crop, set an end date and compare who produced the biggest crop or most fruits or the healthiest plant. It's amazing how competitive people get. This is very involving and lasts a while too. Get a senior manager to judge it.

- Karaoke is great fun and a little less exhibitionist than banging it all out in a bar. Search YouTube for 'karaoke' and you'll find lots of karaoke videos complete with rolling lyrics displayed on the screen. Either share the YouTube screen in the videoconference or better still use one of the video sharing apps like Watch2Gether or TwoSeven to make sure you all synchronise and then you can watch your colleagues put heart and soul into their performances over the video link.

- Come dine with me. Pick a (preferably simple) recipe off an internet food site, order the ingredients in and then prepare and eat it together. Hard to do without a laptop given you need to be mobile, moving from kitchen to dinner table, but good fun if you can make it work and you can involve family members too!

- You might want to offer employees activities like Yoga, Tai Chi, Pilates or Zumba and fund an instructor. Activities like

Zumba are good because they're fun, involving and everyone has the chance to make a fool of themselves! All will work over a remote link.

- Foreign language conversational groups work well over remote links too and can also help integrate teams where different languages are spoken.

You can find even more ideas online. You'll need to experiment to get the balance right, but if you want to pull your team more closely together then I'd strongly recommend trying some of these.

Help everyone settle in

It's always hard when you join a new organisation. It's doubly hard if you work remotely and it's very easy to get lost in the new organisation and start to despair. So think about how you're going to get new people joining your team up and running as quickly as possible.

- Have an induction pack for the project and set up a chat followed by a question and answer session.

- Store all of the project documentation in a single shared location. This is good practice anyway and if you use a project management tool that may well facilitate this.

- Have an up to date organisational chart

- Make it clear who you ask for what on the project.

Meetings

As a remote project manager, meetings are your lifeblood. They're where you talk to your team and really understand what's going on.

Some project management software suppliers would like you to believe that remote or collaborative project management can all be achieved through their tool with its superb communication functionality. They'll happily tell you that you don't need to talk to people because you can do everything through their software. Don't believe a word of it, this is a recipe for isolation and disaster. Talk to people and keep a strong finger on the pulse of what's going on.

In an office environment people pop around to your desk for a chat as a way of resolving issues quickly and keeping you informed. Communication is more fluid and you're less likely to miss something. In a remote situation the opposite is true. To counter this I'd strongly recommend short daily meetings of no more than half an hour duration where everyone can air issues and you can keep track of progress. Daily 'stand-ups' are one of the basic principles of the Agile development methodology where everyone in the meeting quite literally stands up. The meetings are meant to be short, so the idea behind everyone standing up is to make sure they don't get too comfortable. I've seen meeting rooms with no seats, just leaning bars, designed with this in mind. Of course when you're working in a remote team standing up often isn't a great idea or the camera may be trained on your midriff! However, the principle of frequent short meetings is good.

Agile employs a simple agenda for its stand-ups – what did you do yesterday, what are you planning to do today and what impediments are you encountering. This won't work for every remote project, but it's not a bad starting point. I keep an action list that I run through at these meetings to check no-one has forgotten what they'd previously committed to do.

I'd also recommend that you extend one of these meetings to one hour as a formal team meeting to track against the project plan and examine current risks and issues. You can tune the durations of all of these meetings depending on the size of the project and your experience of what is required but I'd definitely recommend short daily meetings.

You also need to think about disseminating information and keeping everyone apprised of the wider project, so I'd recommend a fortnightly slideshow at one of the longer daily meetings where you do just that. Whether you're working remotely or not, don't underestimate the power of this. Everyone welcomes being kept informed about the bigger picture and it may also make it easier to put things into context when difficult decisions need to be made.

Consider getting everyone together for regular meet-ups. Lots of companies organise meet-ups to get their remote and office based employees physically together. These are often badged 'Hackathons', a term that was originally about computer programmers getting together to hack out code but now seems to have been adopted more generally for these sort of business get-togethers. Clearly covering travel and hotels costs can make this an expensive event but I'd recommend it and the chances are you'll make your money back by improving teamwork and generating ideas to help everyone work better. Typically these are held two or three times a year. There's no reason why you can't do this for project teams. If you have the budget then organise a team Hackathon. Teams working in creative industries are especially likely to profit from this given the importance of being able to bounce ideas back and forth between team members.

Review how it's going

Given the added uncertainties in managing a project remotely, I'd strongly recommend that you get your team together regularly during the project to review how things are going. This can nip potential issues in the bud and even point to things that you've fallen into a habit of doing that no-one has had the courage to suggest you stop.

It's good practice in any project to get together to review what's working and what's not. This is often referred to as a lessons learned meeting which is typically held at the end of a project or in Agile as a sprint retrospective which is held at the end of every 'sprint' i.e. chunk of work. It's important in these reviews to encourage everyone to be open and to avoid defensive feelings. Make sure everyone knows they're there to identify what's going well and what's going badly so that you can improve the way that the project is working.

These meetings need to be managed carefully to avoid bruised egos and clashes of opinion, but if done well they can be both instructive and enjoyable.

Look after yourself

Project management jobs can be stressful in an office environment, but can feel even more pressured when you're working remotely. If you're anxious and worn down by your work this won't help you deliver or do anything to enhance your team's performance and morale. You need to make sure that you look after yourself.

Isolation, loneliness and stress

This may sound a bit alarmist but it's something you need to consider particularly if you're working from home.

You're not going to have the same level of support organisation around you that you'd expect to have in an office based set up. This can be difficult to handle and lead to feelings of isolation.

Loneliness is an acknowledged issue for home workers and tends to be exacerbated by long and potentially anti-social hours. The Epson Ecotank Survey of 1000 freelancers[10] found that while there were plenty of positives expressed for working from home, 48% of those interviewed said they had experienced loneliness and 46% said that it was isolating. In addition 29% said they missed being part of a team and 32% missed the social aspects of being in an office. For some people in repetitive jobs a large part of their job satisfaction comes from meeting people and social interaction.

From my experience of working remotely, I've found it's easy to slip into feelings of uncertainty about what value you're adding. I've found myself thinking that doing my job well wasn't enough and feeling pressure to be seen to be always making an impact. My way of compensating for that was to work harder, to try to do a better job than I ever would have face-to-face. In most work situations our performance is rated against our peers. One of the issues with remote work is that often there is no clear benchmark, making it much harder to measure your effectiveness against others doing similar jobs. These and similar behaviors are easy to fall into as a remote worker and can result in overwork, anxiety and stress.

Boundaries between work and leisure have a tendency to blur. With the commute gone and the work computer in the next room there's a strong temptation to keep working or to squeeze a couple of hours of work in before bedtime or at the weekend, particularly if you're up against a deadline. This is exacerbated further if you're working on an international project when you may be called into meetings late at night for you but midday for everyone else. One of the projects I managed involved a meeting that included European, Middle and Far Eastern and an Australian attendee. The Australian attendee always used to joke that he was attending in his pyjamas, because of the time differences. All of this can take a toll on sleep patterns and mental health.

The main thing is to be aware that there is a danger of increased stress, isolation and loneliness. I'd suggest you:

- Be kind to yourself, acknowledge this is a stressful situation and don't beat yourself up if things go wrong

- Work on your social life. Make sure your social life outside of work is as good as you can make it. Get out of the house, meet people, do things, have fun!

- Stay fit. Fitness is important and if you pick the right sport, also a social outlet. I play a lot of tennis and try to make sure I fit my work schedule around my tennis life when I'm working remotely. Exercise relaxes you and boosts endorphins and is a real antidote to being stuck at home all day working. A long walk, a run or a bike ride is good.

- Look after your body. Maybe fitness is a step too far if you're not an active sort of person, but be aware what hours slumped over a laptop can do to your body. This applies to office work too, but in the quieter, more absorbed atmosphere of remote work, it's a lot easier to just obsessively plough on. Staying seated at a desk for hours on end can give you back and neck ache and generally screw your body up. Getting up and walking around frequently is good advice. A study from Columbia University[18] recommended getting up from your desk every 30 minutes. They found that switching out 30 minutes of sedentary time over the course of the day for 30 minutes of low-intensity activity reduced the risk of an early death by about 17%. You might also want to look at Yoga or Pilates as a way of stretching the wrinkles out of your body. What you put into your body also counts, drink plenty of water and if working at home makes you snack more then buy in some healthy snacks rather than loading up on fat, sugar and salt.

- Look after your mind. Bill Gates and Paul McCartney are two amongst many who meditate every morning and swear by its benefits. Twenty minutes meditation before throwing yourself into your day's work starts you off feeling calm and clear minded and provides a break between home life and work life. It's too easy when you're managing remotely to wake up with your head full of thoughts about work, rush through breakfast and just get stuck into it. Think of it as replacing your highly stressful commute with some moments of calm and inner peace. I'd highly recommend Quiet The Mind by Matthew Johnstone as a short and amusing way of learning how to meditate[17].

- Be aware of 'Zoom Fatigue'[16]. From research carried out by Gianpiero Petriglieri, and Marissa Shuffler you're more likely to experience fatigue on videoconferences because the brain has to work a lot harder. Petriglieri observes that not only is it much harder to relax into conversation naturally but we're also constantly trying to try to find the non-verbal content that we usually just absorb without having to think about it. Our minds are together but our bodies are not. Shuffler points out that seeing yourself and also seeing everyone apparently staring at you when you talk can also make you feel like you're constantly performing and that can be exhausting too. Their remedy is to avoid loading yourself with back-to-back video meetings and try turning the camera off if you feel too observed.

- Make use of the flexibility. Working from home gives you flexibility, so take advantage of this. Give yourself a lunch-break, go for a walk, watch some TV or maybe part of a film each day or enroll in a daytime class where you can switch off and meet people. Make sure you're not tied to a desk all day every day for hours on end. It's not good for you, your team or the project

- You might want to consider working in a shared physical space to increase your opportunities for social interaction. This could be a coffee shop with Wi-Fi (as long as security isn't compromised) or one of the many co-working spaces that are springing up aimed mainly at one person businesses. Check out a Jelly – you'll find them online and on Eventbrite. The concept is to get remote workers together to work and collaborate (but not feel pressured to sell) in a shared place at no cost to the user.

- Know when to stop work. One of the biggest issues with home workers is that they don't know when to stop and can end up working long days and weekends, risking stress and burnout.

- Get enough sleep. Just because the office is so close to your bed it doesn't make it a good idea to go straight from the one to the other! Give yourself a decent gap between work and going to bed. The overstimulation associated both with work and staring at screens close to bed time is likely to result in disturbed sleep. You may also want to take advantage of the flexibility of remote work by taking a nap during the day – it's amazing how much this can recharge your batteries, but make sure you set an alarm if you do. "Sorry I missed our team meeting because I fell asleep" really isn't a good line.

Your home office

If you're going to make remote working work for you then you need to have a decent home office. It may initially seem ok to work from the kitchen table but for a whole host of reasons that's likely to become difficult to sustain. Working with any set-up where the screen isn't at eye level is highly likely to result in neck, shoulder and back pain and if continued can cause permanent damage to your health.

There will be times where you'll need privacy or to demonstrate it to the other people on the call. Other members of your family or your cat wandering in and out of shot won't exactly help.

The best environment is one where you can cut yourself off mentally and physically from your home life. As well as providing privacy, this also achieves a level of separation that helps discourage you from merging home and work life. If you don't have this then you should think hard about whether you can make remote working work for you long term.

Once you have your home office you need to be able to set yourself up to facilitate working from home. A decent wide desk so you can have everything you need in front of you, an ergonomic chair with plenty of adjustment to give you proper back and neck support.

Ideally you want a wireless mouse and keyboard and a monitor that you can have at head level – the top third of the screen should be at eye level, the keyboard and mouse at elbow height with your back straight, not hunched over the screen.

You'll probably be spending a good proportion of your working life videoconferencing. Wearing a headset for hours on end can be very tiring and starts to heat your head up. There are lightweight headsets which are better but the set up I prefer is a high quality webcam with a good microphone and the sort of lightweight headphones you'd use for listening to music. There are plenty of good webcams out there and lots of video reviews on YouTube but I'd personally recommend a midrange Logitech or Microsoft webcam. You generally get what you pay for and the cheaper webcams either have poor microphones or poor cameras or both!

Try to make your home office as pleasant and light an environment as possible within the constraints of what's you can do in your home. If you're going to spend all or most of your working life in your home office then you'd better like being there!

Self-esteem and morale

I talked a lot about body language and the frustrations and difficulties that arise because of the lack of earlier, but there are other aspects of remote working that can start to gnaw away at your feelings of self-esteem.

Meetings can be a very different experience. Videoconferencing doesn't lend itself well to working out when you can break in or to warding people off who are trying to talk over you in a meeting. It's much easier to sense the time to either interrupt or to not break in from people's body language in face-to-face meetings. Sometimes video calls can dissolve into a cacophony of noise as several people try to break in at the same time while someone is already speaking. This can be both frustrating and morale draining, but it's important to see this as limitations of the technology and the general situation and not let it get you down.

Think about how you want to appear to the other participants in the videoconference. You see yourself on the screen in videoconferences and it's very easy to start thinking what an unkempt wreck you look and how the camera seems to be exaggerating all of your wrinkles and making you look older than you are. Just because you can roll out of bed straight into your office there's no reason to look like that just happened. You may want to dress smartly and fix your hair and face, plus very importantly sort out the lighting in your office. Most people look pretty ghastly when lit from the side. Face-on lighting makes you look a whole lot better and has a tendency to mask your imperfections (assuming you have any!). Also aim to have the camera at eye level. Below doesn't really work unless you like the Bohemian Rhapsody effect and above doesn't tend to present the best image of you either. If the camera is on top of the screen and hard to move, this may mean you moving instead by changing your chair adjustment during videoconferences. This may all sound a bit facile but don't underestimate it. If you look good then you feel good and when you're working remotely, it's important to keep your moral high.

Key recommendations in how you manage

- You'll need to work harder than you would in a face-to-face environment to keep on top of things
- If you're going to build credibility you need to be very organised
- Make sure you have all of the facts at your fingertips - if you're working in an unfamiliar subject area, carry out your own research to get up to speed
- Show your face - try to avoid voice-only calls
- Put a lot effort into teamwork and communication
- Think about organising remote social events and about how you're going to help everyone settle into the team
- Hold short daily meetings of no more than half an hour where everyone can air issues and you can keep track of progress
- Try to organise a Hackathon where you get everyone together face-to-face - particularly if you're working in the creative industries
- Look after yourself. If you're not functioning well then project delivery and team morale will suffer
- You're going to spend your working life in your home office so make it as pleasant as you can achieve.

Country specifics

Language, time zones, working hours and legal variances all add to the challenge

Language and time zones

Make sure you have a plan for handling language differences. The collaboration and coordination software market is moving towards providing language translation in videoconferencing and instant messaging and decent services already exist for document translation. None of these translations are ever going to be 100% accurate but as mentioned before, with Artificial Intelligence moving into this area, the quality of translation is likely to improve dramatically in the near future.

If you don't or can't have automated translation facilities then consider how you are going to compensate. Do you need to employ a translator? If so has this been allowed for in your project costs and how easy will it be to find someone who may need to have technical skills or understanding in the area you're working in as well as a fluent command of two or more languages?

Time zones can be a real nightmare. Just try arranging meetings (as I have) between three people, one in Europe, one Australia and the other in the Western USA. There's no way you can do this and not have someone working in what would either be their sleeping or leisure time.

This is something you need to get used to if you're working across time zones. You're going to have to accept an increasing blurring of work and leisure hours.

Working hours

While working hours tend to extend or become distorted particularly if you're working across time zones, there may also be more fundamental differences in working hours.

The local working day can vary across the world. Countries within the same time zone may have differing working hours depending on how close they are to the equator. Work in hotter countries tends to start much earlier in the day and finish in early afternoon or be split by a long midday break when the sun is at its hottest.

The working week may differ too, for instance while Europe, Japan and the US work Monday to Friday, much of the Islamic world works on Sundays but not on Fridays.

Public holidays will vary both in their frequency and place in the calendar. I worked with a company in the US and I think they were fairly shocked by the number of public holidays I had against the very few that they had. This can make things difficult and can also result in pressure on you to appear at meetings that happen to fall in public holidays in your country.

There may also be times of the year when staff may be thin on the ground. School holidays in the UK start in July and continue until early September. Most employees with children will take a two week holiday during that period. This is the case in many countries, but of course the dates will differ. You need to be aware if key staff are planning to be on holiday just when you're most likely to need them.

Legal restrictions

What's legal in your country may not be legal elsewhere. For instance I was working with an application that we had installed right across the world but found because of variance in data protection laws, there were some countries where we were unable to deploy it. Once again it's a case of not making assumptions. Good project managers avoid unpleasant surprises, ask questions early and avoid these sorts of issues later.

Key Recommendations in Country Specifics

- Make sure you have a plan for handling language differences
- If you're working across time zones you're going to have accept an increasing blurring of work and leisure hours
- Be aware of differences in working hours and days and times of year that resources may not be available in other countries
- Be aware of legal differences. What's legal in your country may not be legal elsewhere.

3

TECHNOLOGY

Technology overview

The technology needs to facilitate both collaboration between members of a team and the co-ordination of the team by a project manager

There is a host of technology available to facilitate remote working and it's an area that's experiencing explosive growth.

The two words that cover the technology are collaboration and co-ordination. It should facilitate collaboration between members of a team and the co-ordination of the team by a project manager. The market is positively overrun with a wealth of tools that will allow you to achieve both collaboration and co-ordination of geographically dispersed teams but very few that hit everything you're going to need in a single package.

So how do geographically dispersed teams work together? Well they're going to need some way of talking to each other, so that's where videoconferencing comes in. They might need to send messages to each other, so e-mail and instant messaging is useful. Then they'll need to share files so some sort of shared workspace is pretty handy and finally the team will need to co-operate and work to plans which is what project management software is designed to facilitate.

The good news is that all of this is well provided for by a wide choice of software vendors. The bad news is that there are an awful lot of them – project management package vendors alone run into the hundreds and there are growing numbers of instant messaging and videoconferencing packages to choose from. However, storage for shared workspaces is a fairly mature market where making a choice should be reasonably straightforward.

And if you thought all of that was bad, once you start looking a bit closer you find that there is a huge degree of overlap between these tools. Many project management packages provide chat boards, instant messaging and shared storage and have very close integrations with e-mail. Many of the videoconferencing packages include chat and many of the instant messaging applications are also set up to facilitate topic or project based chat boards.

My feeling is that longer term, mergers and partnerships will result in a consolidation into a single market for 'collaboration and co-ordination' tools which will include shared spaces, project management, instant messaging, chat boards and videoconferencing. The big vendors like Microsoft and Google are already moving solidly in that direction.

The main consideration for the selection of any package should be best of breed. As things stand, you are likely to find that buying one package for collaboration and co-ordination won't work because the one that does everything isn't best of breed for any one aspect of its functionality. Comprehensive and least worst might not be what you're after! However if you've already invested in a package from one vendor then you may be tempted to buy the rest from them too. This is likely to be the simplest approach but not necessarily the best or most future-proofed.

This chapter is organised into:

- Communication Technology – covering videoconferencing, messaging and e-mail

- Project and Task Management Tools – a description of what types of tools are available and what they'll do for you

- Buying Project and Task Management Tools – what features to look out for when buying one of these tools

- Shared Workspaces – cloud based file storage

Communication technology

A good videoconferencing set up is a key factor in productivity and teamwork in a distributed project team. Every dollar spent on videoconferencing is money well spent and the more you spend the better your communication will work

Introduction

In this section we'll cover videoconferencing, instant messaging, chat boards and e-mail.

As mentioned earlier a lot of this technology has overlaps. For instance most instant messaging software tools provide chat boards as well as voice and video messaging. Videoconferencing software usually comes bundled with instant messaging. Your main concern should be to source the best of breed in each category and make sure that each package you buy has a good level of integration with everything else.

Videoconferencing

The proliferation of employees working at home combined with headsets, and webcams appearing at nearly every desk gives most company's management the belief that they are set up for videoconferencing. It's also common to see rooms set up as videoconferencing rooms with just a hi-res camera and a couple of decent microphones. In the most basic sense these facilities can be used for videoconferencing but if you want videoconferencing to really work, you'll need to do a lot better than this.

I can't stress enough how important a good videoconferencing set up is to productivity and teamwork in a distributed team. Every dollar spent on videoconferencing rooms is money well spent and the more you spend the better your communication will work. Good videoconferencing kit includes a smart camera that zooms in on the speaker – not just one that shows a wide view of the room where you can barely make out faces. It has high resolution cameras, and screens and good quality sound. Just about every software vendor will support 1080p high resolution images but the some will give you 4K resolution which provides stunning video images. When you use these facilities you feel like you're talking to a real person and not to a grainy image of a room with some anonymous people sat in it. This is important, humans are built for social interaction and to pick up subtleties of body language and facial expression. In many of these facilities, this is totally lost.

While there is a proliferation of videoconferencing software, it all does pretty much the same job. Each of the packages has strengths and weaknesses but the biggest difference you'll make to the experience is how much you invest in the hardware. Good quality cameras are a little more expensive but are vastly superior to the cameras built into laptops and webcams selling for $30 or less. They will produce good images even in low light, include autofocus, have a wide field of view and are able to zoom in or out without losing quality. The better webcams will have dual microphones and capture good quality sound. If you look on Amazon and you'll find a huge choice of webcams, but personally I wouldn't look further than Microsoft, Logitech or Poly and don't go for the lowest priced models.

Videoconferencing requirements for internet bandwidth aren't arduous but remember that if you're sharing a line with other users then your broadband speed will drop significantly. Because of the way videoconferencing works both download and upload speeds are important. You should have at least 2 Mbps download and 1 Mbps upload speeds to get a decent connection with 1080p resolution. This bandwidth requirement does increase slightly the more users you have on a call but this shouldn't be an issue unless you're using Skype which has been described as being to video conferencing as a go-kart is to a sports car and does use more bandwidth the more participants you have on a call.

In a recent role I hosted a weekly meeting with invitees from 8 countries. We used Zoom, but it could have been just about any desktop videoconferencing package. Given issues with bandwidth to get decent audio reception we had to cut the video. I also found that I had to have the sound on maximum to just about work out what the representatives from some countries were saying. This isn't a great medium for getting stuff done especially when you mix in the lack of any real sense of interaction because of the poor technology. As a remote project manager this scenario is a real threat to you doing your job well, especially when you take into account that you may be communicating with people whose first language isn't the same as yours.

I worked for a bank who subcontracted work to an IT company in India. We spent the first six months of the work speaking to the supplier on telephone conference calls. The lines were poor and so was the equipment being used and the results were terrible. I was losing patience with and confidence in the supplier until we installed a good videoconferencing facility. Suddenly I was talking to real people not some distant voice on a phone and our relationship and understanding was transformed. This is a particularly important concern for suppliers who are doing business around the world. Good videoconferencing facilities will help with selling, supply and support.

Videoconferencing is absolutely key for geographically dispersed teams. Often quite complex work is distributed across a team in different locations. In this environment the communications software has to be a facilitator not an inhibitor.

Content sharing and white boards

All videoconferencing packages incorporate screen sharing but not all allow you to share a single window or application rather than the entire screen. Being able to share a single window reduces the chance that you'll accidentally broadcast something you don't want the whole meetings to view. You may be thinking 'so what?' but accidentally broadcasting commercially sensitive or private information could land you in a whole heap of trouble.

If you're in the creative industries and find whiteboards useful then there are plenty of vendors who support shareable interactive white boards which try hard to replicate the meeting room experience.

Of course if you've purchased a camera with a wide enough field of view and that has zoom capabilities, you can share an actual whiteboard rather than a virtual one.

Webinars, training and recording

With companies and employees becoming more distributed, videoconferencing has become an increasingly popular tool for webinars and company Town Hall meetings. Many sales organisations like to use webinar facilities to sell to new clients and engage existing ones. If this is important to you then find out if the tool supports these and in particular how many concurrent users are supported.

In a similar vein, you may want to use videoconferencing facilities for remote training and learning. This should be a very similar set up to running webinars.

You may also be able to make use of break-outs in both training and webinars. This gives the person who calls the meeting the facility to set up virtual break-out rooms with two or more attendees from the main meeting and then have them rejoin the meeting at a later point.

You should also look at the recording facilities offered. As well as being able to record Town Halls, training sessions and live webinars for distribution and later viewing, it can be very useful to record contractual discussions or to be able to provide customers with a recording of a demo by videoconference.

Mobility and voice-only

Many of these packages support a variety of devices from desktop PCs to mobile devices including laptops, tablets and smart phones. These devices are likely to run a variety of operating systems and variants and versions of those operating systems.

This can become quite complex as many tools want to download a desktop client or browser add-on for the best quality and flexibility. This is fine as long as it works on all of your devices and browsers. If you do need to support a wide variety of devices then check that at a minimum the videoconferencing software will work in a browser without an add-on and check which browsers and versions it supports. There's also nothing worse, and I've experienced this myself, than arriving on time for a meeting, trying to log into the meeting only to find out the videoconference you've been invited to uses a package that wants to download a client on to your computer. After ten minutes and a lot of fiddling around you finally make the meeting, late and in a newly wound up state!

If your team is mobile as well as remote then it may be important to be able to include a participant in the meeting who is travelling. Voice-only is likely be very important in this respect so that participants can dial into the meeting using conventional telephony.

I have several times been involved in meetings where at least one participant was in their car and dialing in hands-free. Maybe not the best idea for safety but it's a useful facility for busy people and particularly where people are working in different time zones where your midday might be in the middle of someone else's commute. The dial-in number should be toll-free regardless of what country the person is calling from.

Quality

Quality is king in the videoconferencing world. Get the best quality videoconferencing set up that you can afford.

Desktop licences for videoconferencing packages like Skype for Business/Microsoft Teams, Zoom, Lifesize, Bluejeans, Lark, LogMeIn, Cisco Webex and many more are relatively cheap and a high quality webcam, speakers and/or headset won't set you back very much either. Camera/screen resolution should as a minimum support 1080p but you may want to consider 4K. Most new laptops have 4K capable screens.

If you're going to set up videoconferencing facilities in house then look at companies like Poly (formerly Polycom) and Logitech who have been in the business of improving video and audio conference quality for decades. They existed long before the current proliferation of desktop software packages were even imagined. Their systems integrate with the leading videoconferencing software packages so you can run videoconferences with people coming in from multiple sources. These set-ups better emulate a meeting where everyone is around a table in the same room. The smart cameras provided will rotate and zoom in on the person talking rather than hearing a voice emitting from a distant video of a group huddled around a table. Every CEO should have this quality of facility in their office. If you're having trouble convincing your management to spend money on better quality facilities, then set up a side-by-side demo and the objections will quickly fade. Entry level systems aren't that expensive, so please have a look at what is available.

Huddles

Creating a number of 'huddles' i.e. small videoconference rooms with good videoconferencing facilities is an excellent arrangement. This will transform how you connect with your team, suppliers and customers. You don't have to make a decision between huddles or providing employees with a cheap videoconferencing package on their desktops. The two should complement each other and provide flexibility when an employee isn't in the office or is asked to dive impromptu into a meeting already underway.

Administration and Reporting

Most packages offer reporting for call, device and feature usage and quality of service performance. They'll also provide a detailed breakdown of usage by user.

There are a variety of set-up options available in different packages. Some e.g. Lark use voice recognition to provide subtitling. It's common that the software switches the screen to the person talking but some offer that as an option. Pretty much all offer recording as an option but not often with their free versions. Some e.g. Zoom provide accessibility features to vary the on screen font sizes. If virtual backgrounds turn you on then that's a common feature too, done particularly well by Microsoft Teams right now. Having your video window always on top is also a nice feature if you're say working through a problem on a call and need to flit around other windows to find the solution. Several e.g. Cisco Webex provide this.

Videoconferencing package vendors

There is no shortage of videoconferencing packages. These come from suppliers who have started from different places in the software marketplace. Some are selling office applications and have added videoconferencing into their collaboration toolset e.g. Microsoft Skype/Teams and Google Hangouts/Meet, some from communications companies e.g. Cisco and Arkadin (NTT) and some from smaller, more agile and innovative players in this market e.g. Zoom, Lark and LogMeIn, Lifesize and Bluejeans.

Be aware that the larger players are trying to tie you into their complete office or communication suites and so are a lot weaker on integration with other collaboration and coordination software whereas by necessity the smaller companies will put greater emphasis on offering a wider range of integrations.

A number of vendors offer free use of their packages on a limited functionality or limited user basis. This is of course an attempt to get you hooked before upselling you a more performant version.

As with many of the other tools we've looked at in this book, there is a proliferation of vendors in this market and some of the smaller ones clearly will not survive or will be gobbled up by other players. While videoconferencing is important, it's probably a little easier to change should your current vendor go out of business than to change your project management package. Even so please check the financial status of the vendor before signing up.

Please check the minimum bandwidth requirements for internet upload and download for your package. These aren't generally arduous but they differ from vendor to vendor and if you need to set up videoconferences where one or more of the participants has poor line speeds then this may be a consideration.

Instant messaging

OK, so far we've talked about videoconferencing, but there are other ways of communicating. You can do this through good old e-mail or through your project management package which may well feature chat boards and web chat or you can use a specialised instant messaging package.

Instant messaging is everywhere. WhatsApp on mobiles has become the world's favourite instant messaging app with over 1.5 billion users at January 2018 and 65 billion messages sent every day. It probably isn't the greatest tool to use for a project team but the principles it works on are not so different to business messaging applications. At a basic level they all support one-to-one chats, group discussions and the inclusion of a wide range of media into the chat stream.

You can see how useful instant messaging can be from the widespread use of WhatsApp by consumer businesses as well as by individuals. Want to get a dent fixed in your car? Just send the dent specialist some images of the bent panel by WhatsApp and they'll send you a quote without ever having seen your vehicle.

Web chat buttons are appearing on lots of websites to help customers to resolve issues or queries and I find them more responsive and a lot less irritating than picking up the phone and having to listen to some inane imitation of music for 10 minutes before I get to talk to someone. Instant messaging applications are also starting to invade the world of medicine with a boom in applications that connect you with a mix of messaging, voice and video to a medical practitioner.

Instant messaging can tie a geographically dispersed team together day-to-day and hour-by-hour. You have to be careful it doesn't become a time consuming distraction, but used properly it's a way of resolving issues quickly and keeping your team communicating.

Business messaging applications usually support a wide range of integrations with office, video conferencing and other third party software and the smarter instant messaging applications are moving towards mixing chat, message boards, voice and video all in the same package.

Can't quite work out what someone is getting at in a text chat? Click and have a quick audio chat with them. This is a really great facility as it helps gets around one of the biggest irritants with remote working which is not being able to have a quick chat to clear the air or sort out an issue without having to arrange a meeting. The type of thing that in an office environment, you'd walk around to their desk to sort out.

The better tools allow you to put a hold or bar on incoming messages for a defined period so you don't have to be plagued by people who want to talk while you're getting on with something that you need to dedicate your full concentration to.

As with all collaboration and co-ordination tools the market is exploding with packages. There are the usual suspects Microsoft, Google and Cisco, but other new small innovative players like Slack, Twist and Discord are starting to gain a real foothold. Of these Slack is the one that has the biggest profile and say they processed 1 billion messages per week in 2019, however Discord which is open source and license-free claims to be processing twice as many. Discord came out of the gaming community and isn't quite so business focussed as Slack. Twist is a genuine competitor to Slack. Of the three Slack has far more off the shelf integrations available including links to e-mail, storage, videoconferencing, project management and programming applications.

Make sure your instant messaging application facilitates group chats as well as one-to-one messaging and that the messages are stored and are both searchable and archivable. Most instant messaging applications also allow you to organise messages by topic, interest area or department similar to chat boards. The facility to produce a transcript from a chat meeting is also useful.

You should be able to load or link to files into your chats and ideally to invite other users of your chat application in other departments or companies into your chat threads.

A number offer password protected group chats if you're worried about someone breaking into a group chat who shouldn't be there.

Make sure there is some level of integration with other applications you plan to use and that messages are encrypted both in flight and at rest.

Messaging is pretty handy for maintaining communication wherever you are, so it's very important that a business messaging package works on a wide variety of devices – from desktop PCs to tablets and mobile phones.

As mentioned earlier most of the messaging applications overlap with the other collaboration and co-ordination tools which may have messaging and chat boards already built in.

Many are free to use but charging starts either once you exceed a number of users or exceed a storage upload limit. Another common limitation with the free versions is to severely restrict access to your message history.

Licence costs are relatively small and charged per user per month for packages hosted in the cloud, but check how much storage this gives you. While chat itself uses very little storage, videos, images and documents included in the chat do, so make sure you won't be hit for an additional charge if you exceed a storage allowance.

E-mail

E-mail has been with us since the 1970s and isn't about to disappear just yet. In many countries including the US e-mails are legally valid and in many respects have replaced mailed letters. They will remain part of the suite of communications tools for some time to come. E-mail overload is a common complaint of project managers and particularly remote project managers. There are some developments that may help with that.

Automation is becoming more available through packages like MixMax which can be set up to automatically schedule meetings, tell you who's read an e-mail you sent and remind those who didn't that you're expecting a reply. MixMax also provides you with a variety of e-mail templates to hopefully help save you time.

A number of the other collaboration and coordination tools integrate with e-mail. For example it's common for project management packages to send e-mail reminders for tasks to be completed and messaging applications often have tight integration with e-mail.

Language translation

I was working recently with a distributed team made up of native English, Spanish and Portuguese speakers. Our conversations were technical and detailed and proved so difficult that eventually we decided to bring a translator into the meetings.

The good news is that this doesn't have to be the case as suppliers are starting to provide the option of language translations in videoconferences, instant messages and chat board applications. The translations are never going to be perfect but should convey the gist of what is being said. If this is important to you, you may want to trial tools that offer this.

Translation will definitely become a more universal feature in time and will improve dramatically as Artificial Intelligence advances further into the world of language translation.

Security

A lot of potentially confidential and/or commercially sensitive information is going to be communicated via the public internet, so instant messages need to be encrypted in transit and your voice and videoconferencing should conform to the current security protocols. You may also want to consider using a Virtual Private Network (VPN), there's more on this in Chapter 4 – Security.

Many videoconferencing and instant messaging packages offer password protected meetings and message groups. If security is a concern then don't buy a package that doesn't provide some sort of meeting ID and a separate password. Don't send people links that bypass the need to include a meeting ID and password, it's too easy a route for intruders to infiltrate the meeting.

Security is important for videoconferencing. The absolute must is end-to-end encryption of video and audio. Most but not all vendors support this. Don't invest in a package that doesn't. Cisco Webex, Skype and BlueJeans all provide end-to-end encryption. Most videoconferencing applications will show who is attending a meeting and some offer the meeting host the facility to mute, block or drop attendees from a meeting and to lock the meeting once everyone has arrived. Look also for packages that play a sound when someone joins or leaves (to avoid unauthorised attendees slipping in unnoticed).

There has been a lot of recent publicity regarding back doors into videoconferencing software allowing hackers to gain control of your computer's camera. This shouldn't be facilitated by any software package. Make sure you probe your supplier closely on the level of security and vulnerabilities in any packages you're looking to buy.

No-one thought too deeply about security when e-mail was invented in the 1970s so one of the downsides with e-mail is that it isn't secure. You may want to invest in a secure e-mail service like Posteo or ProtonMail.

Hosted or on-premise

All vendors offer a hosted service but you may be interested in running videoconferencing and instant messaging on your own servers for performance or security reasons. In this case ask vendors if they support an on-premise deployment, that is one that you deploy on your own servers or data centre.

Key communcation technology recommendations

- Get the best quality videoconferencing set up that you can afford
- Consider buying smart cameras that zoom in on the speaker and high quality screens and audio
- Consider installing 'huddles' – small video conference rooms with high quality equipment
- Instant messaging can tie a geographically dispersed team together and become a way of resolving issues quickly
- Take a look at e-mail automation
- Look for communications packages that integrate easily with other elements of your IT infrastructure
- Language translation will improve dramatically as Artificial Intelligence advances further into the world of language translation
- Make sure messages are encrypted both in transit and at rest and that voice and video conferencing conform to current security protocols.

Project management tools

Until recently Microsoft Project dominated a very small market and if you couldn't afford Microsoft's pricing, then it was down to drawing diagrams in a spreadsheet or resorting to a ruler, paper and a thick pen

Introduction

Until quite recently selecting project management software was something a 10 year old could easily have done. A very small market was dominated by Microsoft Project with few other alternatives available other than resorting to pen and paper.

Those days are long gone, with a flood of project and task management packages coming into the market. At the last count more than 400 packages were available from as many suppliers, resulting in a complex, crowded marketplace.

IDC a global provider of market intelligence, advisory services, and events for the information technology sector forecasts that the global market for project and portfolio management tools will grow at 6.8% per annum from around $4.5 billion in 2017 to $5.7 billion in 2022.

So how will they help me as a remote project manager?

As a remote project manager you're going to have to be able to share plans with your team members. You also need them to be able to log the time they've spent on your project and how complete they think their planned activities are. You'll almost certainly be competing for resources with other project managers in your company. How are you going to check that the skills you need are available when you need them? You're going to need to produce reports for your management too. You're going to be hard pressed to do all of this with a desktop project planner and e-mail.

Modern project management tools are designed to allow you to manage teams regardless of where they're situated. Most also facilitate communication with and between team members through message boards, comments on tasks and instant messaging and allow the sharing and review of documentation. Better still, many will allow you to share plans with your customer and produce project reports virtually at the click of a mouse.

The more sophisticated packages are backed by a relational database, which allows you to use data analysis tools to show any aspect of your project or project portfolio in easily understandable graphical summaries.

The right tool will give also you an executive level view, to be able to run reports that show at a glance the status, financials and delivery dates of each project in the portfolio and trace how they are performing against their original estimates. This is a very powerful tool for transparency and putting management teams in control of their project portfolio.

If you're a project based service company, you'll be able to monitor revenue and profit for each of your projects and for your entire project portfolio on a week-by-week or even day-by-day basis which gives you a high degree of control over your business.

Ultimately they should save you time and help you be more organised and co-ordinated. However, initially you'll need to invest time setting up resources, project templates, training staff, understanding the full capabilities of the package, and agreeing standards for how you're going to use it.

Project based service companies

I'd go as far as saying that this sort of tool is absolutely essential if you're running this sort of business. You'll be able to monitor your profitability and identify your major financial risks on a week by week basis. You'll know which projects look likely to overspend and which ones look like they'll make lots of money. You'll have a week-by-week view of your employee utilisation – a vital number for any resource based business.

More than that the package will impose its own discipline on your employees. Project managers will need to keep their plans up to date and team members their time logged. If they don't you can see it all instantly on the reports you can get from these systems.

There are countless examples of project based service companies getting into trouble with underperforming fixed price contracts. It often seems hard to believe that these companies could have allowed so many contracts to get into difficulties. The better project management tools put company boards back in control. So if you're running a project based service business this sort of package is an investment you'll never regret.

No longer the preserve of big companies

Until recently project management tools have been mainly the preserve of large enterprises, who have been using them for decades. However with software now available via the cloud on a subscription model based primarily on use, their adoption by all types of businesses is increasing very rapidly.

Cloud based

All of these applications are available as a service via the cloud, so you don't need to buy any special infrastructure, just pay your subscription, point your browser to the right place and go.

Most vendors also offer collaboration space in the cloud, where plans and documents can be shared and reviewed and project team members can communicate.

Some vendors also offer on-premise versions for you to install in your datacentre or on a server. On-premise gives you added flexibility and security and it's also not uncommon to see vendors offering wider functionality for on-premise versions than the hosted versions. You'll usually pay a one off license based on the number of users and an annual maintenance fee thereafter. But also be aware that in some cases there may be an additional service charge to ensure your installation is kept in line with the hosted version.

Any device anywhere

All of the packages will give you access through a browser and many through a mobile app, allowing you to access project data, time sheets etc. through pretty much any device at just about any location.

Subscription based

Another common theme in this market is that like most cloud based software, these tools are subscription based. This is usually by a monthly charge although most vendors want you to sign up for a minimum of a one year term and either make this a contractual requirement or offer you a considerable financial incentive to do so.

Nearly all vendors offer a free 14 or 30 day trial and some a totally free limited functionality configuration of their package as a taster to tempt you into their paying versions.

Not a commodity market

If you thought all of these packages were basically the same, you'd be very wrong. Packages offer differing functionality and varied pricing and it's important to fully understand both what is on offer and what you want before buying. Price isn't always a reliable guide to how good or functionally rich these tools are. There are some terrible deals and some bargains available. As always, understanding what you're buying is key and particularly with these packages, the devil is in the detail.

Not a single market

There are a variety of packages out there. Some try to be all things, some to carve out niches. But as a general rule I'd split the market into 5 sections:

1. Specialist Agile Project Management Tools

2. Low End Project Management Tools

3. Standard Project Management Tools

4. High End Project Management Tools

5. Large Enterprise Level Tools.

In case you haven't heard of it, Agile is a methodology used primarily by IT teams to develop software in a more flexible, user focused way. The Agile tools are tailored to that methodology and while it is possible to use Agile for any application, it is predominantly used for IT projects. These tools are specialised for that market but vary from cheap tools that can maintain a backlog and support running sprints to comprehensive tools that support running a portfolio of Agile projects. Examples of Agile tools are Jira, Axosoft, Assembla, Target Process and Spiraplan.

The Low End Tools allow task management, with minimal reporting capabilities. Most offer some collaboration functionality and in fact many are more collaboration tools with a bit of project management than out-and-out project management tools. There is a very wide variance in price for this class of tools, but more often than not, that variance is not reflected in delivered functionality. Examples of Low End Tools are Asana, Basecamp, Monday and Trello, but Jira also appears in this camp as it can be used more generally for project management as well as for Agile. Many of these tools have an open architecture and encourage third parties to build add-ons to expand their core functionality.

Standard Project Management Tools support all of the functions you would expect to see in a project management package. They all have capable task management, all support Gantt views, all allow time recording and most will show actuals against estimated. They all have decent reporting and most fully support financials. Again the variance in price in this class of tools can be dramatic. The other thing to note about the better tools in this market is that they're for obvious reasons trying to match the functionality of the high end tools without creeping too far into their pricing range, so some real bargains are available here. The sort of tools I'd classify here are EasyProjects, Wrike, Liquid Planner, Smartsheet and Zoho Projects.

The High End Project Management Tools support everything you get in a standard tool but in a more comprehensive and usually very flexible way. They will often include the ability to build processes and to capture and manage risks and issues, and track change. These tools will support your business regardless of what size it grows to. Some are tailored to specific businesses e.g. service companies, some are more suitable for in-house teams. Most are moving to storing all project data in a relational database and offering Business Intelligence (BI) tools to provide sophisticated graphical reports from this data. They are just below the Enterprise Level Tools sold by the likes of Oracle and Hewlett Packard, but not by much. Once again pricing can vary dramatically, without any real increase in value. The sort of tools I'd classify here are Microsoft Project Online, Cora, Mavenlink KeyedIn and Clarizen.

Enterprise Level Tools are costly and aimed at very large companies. These packages are more likely to run on a large company's own IT infrastructure than in the cloud and are highly integrated with other tools provided by that vendor. Examples of these are Hewlett Packard's PPM and Oracle Primavera PPM.

Changing your mind might be more difficult than you think

If you're thinking because these tools are subscription based, that if the package doesn't turn out to be right for you then you can easily move on....think again!

Despite offering a monthly subscription, more and more tools are mandating a minimum one year term, so you'll be committed to a whole year's outlay. This isn't a nasty sales trick, it's mainly because of the overheads involved in both setting you up and maintaining you as a new customer on their hosted service and also because in an increasingly competitive market companies are finding they need a year's subscription to cover the cost of their sales effort.

Most of the Standard and High End Tools will offer you a start-up package. This involves analysing how you do things now, configuring the package to your needs and then training your employees in this configuration. This is a great idea. I've come across a number of companies who thought that buying a project management package would solve all of their delivery problems and then sadly found it made virtually no difference. It isn't just about the package, it's also about how you use it and the processes you build around it. Done well, this start-up phase will challenge you to determine how you're going to use the software effectively and consistently. However, there will be an additional one-off charge for this.

Even if you pick a Low End Tool, you'll still invest a huge amount of time into making it work for you. You'll train staff, build standards, build plans and resource profiles into it and start filling it up with project documents, messaging threads and review comments. Vendors know this, which is why many offer subscription free starter packages.

It becomes a very difficult decision to change once you've purchased a package and started to use it. I've worked with companies who have purchased what have turned out to be poor value tools, with significant deficiencies, but even so were very resistant to make a change because of the effort involved and that they were simply too busy.

One of the companies I know bought a tool that didn't include employee time tracking, so rather than change to a package that did, they found it less hassle to buy a separate time recording system and then try to link them together. Another struggled with the way the package scheduled activities and found that it didn't support the notion of a fixed price project very well, which given they were an IT shop, wasn't great.

It's easy to be critical but it really isn't easy to get this right and you're likely to be committing to a significant investment once you add the start-up charges to the annual fees and training time for your own staff. These are complex pieces of software, so take your time choosing the right package for you. Get your due diligence right. You might want to think about trying to find a consultant who knows this market well to help you through this stage of the process. A couple of months spent deciding what you want, looking into the detail and checking out a few packages will save you a lot of money and heartache later.

So will these packages solve all of my project delivery issues?

Well as we've said earlier, if you're running a remote team then these packages aren't even an option, they're essential. However while they will help you run your projects, they're not the route to an eternally happy life that some vendors' websites would have you believe. They're not going to turn poor project managers into faultless geniuses who always deliver on time and budget.

However a modern project management package, if used correctly, can be a first transformative step towards making projects in your company run more effectively. These packages provide good facilities for project teams to produce plans and keep them up to date, capture time worked, optimise staff utilisation, capture and track financials, monitor project status and publish project status reports.

Most importantly they facilitate executive level reporting. Reports from the tool will provide executives with data to allow them to ask penetrating questions and create pressure to ensure that projects are being run appropriately. But don't expect to buy one and instantly transform your project delivery. To do that you need to have trained staff, well thought out and documented project management processes and to structure your company to support project delivery, as well as selecting the right package for your needs.

Key project management tools recommendations

- A modern project management tool isn't an option for remote project management it's essential. It will facilitate managing teams wherever they're located
- There are hundreds of tools available with a wide range of capabilities - no two are the same. This is definitely not a commodity market
- Changing is not easy once you've started using a tool, so take time and care to carry out due diligence and pick the right package
- Make sure the tool you choose gives you an executive level view and reports that show the status, financials and delivery dates of each project in your portfolio
- If you're a project based service company, the package you choose should be capable of monitoring the revenue and profit of projects on a week-by-week or even day-by-day basis
- Most tools are cloud and subscription based but if it's important to you, on-premise versions are available from many vendors.

Buying a project management tool

The single most important factor in buying anything is to be clear what your requirements are. Get your selection right – choose in haste and repent at leisure!

Introduction

The single most important factor in buying anything is to understand what your requirements are – you wouldn't be at all surprised if you ended up buying the wrong package if you didn't know what you wanted in the first place.

This is especially true if you haven't used a project management tool before, when as often happens in that scenario, the chances are you'll end up learning the hard way, from your mistakes.

This is a complex market place with hundreds of tools available with a wide range of capabilities and as explained earlier buying the wrong tool will be a costly mistake.

Is the vendor here to stay?

Before you start looking at features and functionality, you need to ask a few questions about the potential supplier.

As we've already pointed out, you'll find that project management software isn't just for Christmas, it's for life. Once you start using a package you swiftly become inexorably tied to it. So there are two imperatives:

- Get your selection right
- Pick a product that is going to be around as long as you hope your business will be.

With more than 400 suppliers out there, the only thing that is certain is that a lot of these are either going wind up out of business or will be gobbled up by their rivals.   What seems probable is that the poorer tools, the ones currently overcharging for their delivered functionality and the ones with a low installed base are the most likely to disappear as market growth tails off.   Many vendors are also supported by venture capital and don't have a viable business as yet.

So the important questions are:-

- What is their installed customer base?

- How long they've been in business?

- Can they show you financial results and employee count for the last five years or if not how they are being financed?

- Can they provide you with reference customers with a similar profile to you who you can contact?

Another consideration should the worst happen and your supplier goes out of business is that you still have access to the data that you've stored in the package. Check this out before buying.

How do they support the package?

You'll want to know what standard of support you're going to get once you've purchased the package. Where is support located and what hours and days of the year do they provide support? If they're on the other side of the world, they could be in bed just when the package starts crashing or you desperately need some help to complete a plan for a client. How do you contact support? Is this by logging a support ticket, sending an e-mail or by phone and what sort of response times do they quote for each? Don't underestimate how important one of these packages could become to your business, particularly if you use them to manage projects across a large dispersed team.

Price also comes into this and as well as being related to the functionality of the package is also going to be reflected in the level of support. If you're paying $30 per user per month expect better and more responsive support than if you're only paying $7.

Hosting

All of these packages offer a hosted service, so find out how this is going to work. For a start make sure you're clear about any limitations on storage. Can you have unlimited projects and documents or will your monthly charge be increased once you breach defined storage limits?

All of your plans and project documents are likely to end up being held on a remote server, so you need to know about back-ups and disaster recovery. What happens if there's a flood or other sort of disaster at your supplier's hosting facility? How long will it be before access to your plans and documents is restored? All vendors should have a disaster recovery strategy. Their servers will also be down for routine maintenance at various times, find out when these are and what the historic uptime has been for their facility.

Most vendors will use one of the big hosting service suppliers such as Amazon AWS or Microsoft Azure, but be aware that these hosting suppliers offer a wide range of differently scoped services. Find out what service your supplier has purchased and if it addresses the back-up and disaster recovery concerns we've detailed above.

Performance of the application will also depend on what level of service the package supplier has purchased with their hosting provider. The CPU and disk capacity purchased and the degree of sharing with other users of the hosting facility will affect performance and can cause frustrating delays and time lags.

On-premise

You may for reasons of performance, control or security want to have the package run on your own infrastructure. Most vendors don't support this, but you will find many who do. You may also find you have to pay an additional support charge to keep your version in line with the cloud version. The vendor may also want to do this work rather than you doing it yourself, to minimise any support issues.

Browser and operating system support

Think about how you want to access the software. Check that the browsers, browser versions and mobile devices that you want to use are supported. If Apps are available for mobile devices, will they be supported on the operating systems you want to use?

If the software is only supported in a browser on a mobile device rather than an App, then check it's going to work on the browsers on the mobile devices that you want to use.

Often only a subset of the package's overall functionality is supported on a mobile device. If mobiles are important to you check what functionality is supported on what platform.

Security

This system may hold the keys to your business or a significant part of it. Documentation and plans for all of your future developments are not the sort of thing you want falling into the hands of your competitors, so you should be concerned about security.

Most vendors offer encryption of data in transit, but fewer offer encryption of data at rest. Usually your data is held in a shared instance in a server farm which may not meet your security needs. If it doesn't then ask if you can have your own encrypted instance, but be warned this is usually very expensive and it may be more economic to host the package yourself.

Permission levels are another must-have. You're going to need to be able to define a number of roles with different permissions e.g. Administrator, Manager, User, Customer. Some packages come with set roles, others let you configure role types from a large set of permissions.

You may also want to know about log-on security. Phishing is the single most effective hacking technique. You might want a package that offers two-factor authentication and/or enforces a change of password at defined time intervals. Check what the package's password and security policy is and if this is configurable.

What features do you need?

Clearly it's a good idea to decide what you need before going out and buying anything. With something as feature-rich as a project management package, you would do well to decide not only what you want now, but also what you think you may need in the future.

Many vendors up-sell features on the basic subscription, so be careful you don't buy something that appears to be good value, but turns out not to be when you find you have to pay an increased subscription for something you need. I'd also advise that you don't get seduced too much by a flashy look and feel. Functionality will help you run your projects, not the way it looks.

As we've already said, features don't necessarily equate to price. Some packages are ridiculously overpriced for the functionality that they deliver. Make sure you're paying for the features being delivered, not the vendor's large advertising budget!

Gantt charts

Most but not all tools produce project plans as a Gantt chart, the ubiquitous bar chart representation of a plan, invented by Mr Gantt in the 1920s. Most tools will also show your plan as a list of tasks and increasingly as Kanban boards. I wouldn't feel I had a plan unless I could see a Gantt chart with resourcing, deliverables and dependencies. If you're the same make sure the packages you consider support this.

Dependencies

Being able to set up dependencies between tasks is very important to be able to schedule them properly.

Dependencies are a bit more complex than you might at first think. You should be able to make another task dependent not only on an earlier task finishing, but also on that task starting and be able to offset both, that is 'start task x, n days after task y has started/finished'. This allows you a lot more flexibility than the simple 'start this task when that one has completed' type of dependency that you find in most packages.

Constraints

If you haven't used project management software before, then buying one that has constraints might sound a bit odd. However constraints are handy and add more flexibility to how you can construct your schedules.

There are a number of possible constraints, but the most important ones are:

- That an activity must start by a given date
- Or must end by a given date
- Or must start no earlier than a given date
- Or must finish no earlier than a given date.

Examples of how these would be used are:

- Start by a given date might be used for a seminar, where publicity has gone out and speakers booked, so the 'run the seminar' activity must have a fixed start date, which would also affect the dates of preceding activities
- 'End by a given date' might be used if you know that the only resource with the skills to carry out this activity is about to leave the company or be assigned to another project, so you need to have the activity completed before you lose them
- 'Start no earlier than' is mainly used where there are dependencies on external activities or resources e.g. a supplier completing work that you are dependent on. You may not have to start on a set date, but you know you can't start until the external dependency has been fulfilled
- 'Finish no earlier than' is used in situations where you know a task has to be completed, but you also know there's no rush, so you can use this to schedule it for when it's needed, which might help you with resourcing it.

Levels

In your business you'll probably have a top level of clients or maybe business areas and then projects below that. The projects themselves will then probably break down into sub-projects and tasks. You need your planning software to be able to support this sort of structure.

Resources

You need to be able to put resources into your plans and you may want to add both a cost and a charge rate to each resource. The cost rate for a resource won't vary between projects but the charge rate may well do, so ideally the charge rate should be variable by project and/or customer account. This will allow you to calculate what each project and your portfolio of projects are costing and if you're a service company whether they're in profit or not.

All packages will allow you to allocate employees to your plan but some will also allow you to include physical resources e.g. the costs of renting a building, buying a computer or a software package.

You might think that resourcing is just about allocating free employees to projects, but it's much bigger than that. You need to be able to see who is free when across the whole company resource pool, find resources with the right skills and make sure they're not over allocated once you've assigned them to tasks on your project.

For this, you need to have the ability to associate skills to resources, so that you can look for a free resource with say Java programming skills. You also need a portfolio view so that you can see at a glance which resources are free at what times across the whole company resource pool. With this information you might talk to another project manager to see if a resource you need could be spared for a couple of weeks by adjusting their plan or alternatively move an activity on your plan to accommodate when a resource is free.

You probably want to be able to look ahead to see when resources become free to make sure you're not going to have people sitting around waiting for suitable work. If you're running a development shop then you really want to know when pools of resources, say designers, developers and testers are likely to be over or underutilised so that you can optimise their use. If you're a service company, keeping utilisation of resources high will keep your bottom line healthy. Having people sitting around is bad for morale and bad for your profit margin.

Scheduling

First let's deal with auto-scheduling. By this I mean that a change to project x will automatically change the schedule for project y, if a resource needed by both projects is extended by project x. This is showing the effect in real life, clearly if Bill is wanted by both projects and Bill is extended by project x, then project y can't have him, so it will slip.

However this can make it quite difficult to disentangle what has happened, particularly if several projects and several resources are involved. If I'm running my project particularly well, I'm likely to be a bit shocked when my schedule extends because of something that has happened on another project. It can take significant time and effort to work out what has gone on, especially where several projects and resources are involved. Clearly the overuse of a resource needs to be flagged up, but the alternative is for the project management software to indicate that the resource has become overloaded so that in the example, both project managers see that some action is required. The project managers can then find out why the resource is overloaded and try to sort out the issue.

Both have their plusses, but I wouldn't recommend selecting a package that only auto-schedules. I'd look for one that gives you an option to switch auto-scheduling on or off, to allow you to decide what works best for you. In the end you want to be in control of who is scheduled to do what and when. Having the package decide that for you doesn't feel quite right.

Reminders

Most packages will send out e-mail reminders to staff regarding their current and forthcoming tasks. This reminds staff that they have tasks to complete this week and more tasks coming up the following week.

This is a nice facility, but be careful you don't use it as a substitute for talking to people! It's also easy to find in-trays filling up with reminders, particularly for staff who are working on several projects, so look at how this function can be configured.

Project status reporting

Projects need to be reported on throughout their term, otherwise you can end up finding something is amiss near to the end of the project when it's too late to do something.

One of the real positives with a project management package is that all of the project data is held in the tool, so it should be relatively easy to produce reports from it. The quality and breath of the reporting tends to distinguish the better tools. Project reporting can take up huge amounts of your time. A good project management package should make it easy.

The trend for the better packages is to store all of the data they capture in a relational database so that you can use a Business Intelligence (BI) tool to produce whatever reports you want in numerical or graphical format or both. The power of BI tools is that they allow you to drill down into the data. So for instance a summary showing all projects in the portfolio would allow you at the click of a mouse to drill down into individual project performance or the performance of all projects for one customer or one department or one project manager. A resourcing view of the entire resource pool would allow you to drill down by skill groups or by individual to determine when resources are free and which resources are being over-scheduled and by what projects. You'll usually be provided with a library of predefined reports but after that it's up to you. This is a very powerful and flexible tool allowing you to analyse both individual projects and the entire project portfolio.

Capturing time and spend

A number of packages offer nothing more than scheduling. They'll let you set up task lists and a Gantt chart and assign resources to tasks, but that's about where it ends.

If you're going to be able to track how well your project is doing and in particular what you've spent then you need to be able to capture time. This is typically done by providing an online timesheet for individuals working on a project to record what time they've spent on what activities. An important feature to look out for is approval of this time. Lots of packages only allow the entire timesheet to be signed off by a nominated approver. In the better packages, the manager of each project signs off the time that individuals have spent on their project. This is much more empowering because as project manager you may want to question people's time entries or challenge an entry in error from someone who doesn't even work on your project.

You may also have a need to export timesheet data if you have a customer who wants you to re-enter time spent on their work into their time recording systems. This isn't an uncommon requirement for a service company.

Risks, issues and actions

Monitoring risks, issues and actions are some of the most basic and important jobs that a project manager needs to carry out.

Some packages include being able to register and monitor risks, issues and actions. I wouldn't see this as a high priority requirement, more a nice to have, but it's good to have all of this information in the same place rather than in a collection of spreadsheets.

Change control

All projects need to track change and before you Agile enthusiasts say that's dinosaur Waterfall speak....you're wrong. Something has to be fixed in an Agile project and usually it's budget and timescale (but not functionality).

Scope creep is one of the worst possible scenarios for a project. If you don't control change then your promise to deliver what was required at x cost on y date goes out of the window.

It's less common for project management packages to support change control but some do.

Integrations

All of the Enterprise Level Tools, which are aimed at larger companies, include integrations with other software. This is important to large enterprises, where there is a huge investment in IT infrastructure, but you may also find this of value in your company if for example you want to link to your accounting software to track spending or produce invoices.

Many packages offer integrations to popular software like QuickBooks and Salesforce and most offer an open API (Application Program Interface) which can be used to build an interface with almost any other piece of software, but make sure if you have particular integrations in mind that the vendor can give you guarantees that you can connect.

In addition many of the Low End Tools and some of the Standard Project Management Packages have open architectures where they encourage third parties to produce add-ons to their core software. The Low End Tools tend to have smaller core functionality and then a whole host of add-ons available to both enhance the functionality and interface to other software. A good example of this is Jira. You can buy add-ons for Jira from countless vendors for workflow automation, project management, time recording, invoicing, test management and asset management as well as a whole host of integrations. There are literally thousands of add-ons for Jira. Jira is low priced and the add-ons generally even cheaper or sometimes free, but there is a risk of ending up with a complex array of tools from different vendors that don't work quite as well as a single integrated package. Support can also get tricky where a number of vendors are involved. The Standard Project Management packages tend to be far more feature rich so their add-ons are fewer and focussed on interfacing. A good example of this is Wrike who have less than 50 add-ons which are primarily integrations with office applications, storage providers, e-mail and CRM systems.

Project lifecycle

A number of vendors also try to build some element of project lifecycle into the tool. This is more pronounced with those attempting to support the Agile development methodology. As mentioned earlier there are a number of project management tools that provide explicit support for Agile.

Dashboard

Most packages will allow each user to see a summary dashboard, with their part of the plan, their outstanding actions and reminders, risks and so on. However some packages only give users this view and don't allow them to see the entire project plan unless they have project manager privileges. This matters if they charge more for users with project management privileges, as several vendors do. Microsoft Project online is an example of this. The basic user license doesn't cost a lot but allows only a very limited view of the project plan. Look out for this, it's definitely not helpful for users to only be able to view a small portion of the plan and not the entire plan.

Document storage

Many packages include a built-in document repository. Most will support links to a variety of external document stores e.g. Google Drive, Microsoft SharePoint, Dropbox and Box.

Where a document repository exists it may also support version tracking, that is if you modify a document or upload a new version the package automatically saves the old version. This provides you with security in case someone messes up the current version and an audit trail, should you need to go back over the project's history.

Portfolio management features

Portfolio management is one of the huge positives with using project management software. It will allow you to:

- Monitor progress and costs for your whole portfolio of projects
- Utilise staff efficiently
- Forecast your ability to bid for or start new work
- Know what your entire portfolio of projects is costing you
- If you're a service company to understand the revenue and profitability of your entire project portfolio on a week-by-week basis.

Given all of the data for your projects is held in the project management package, producing reports for portfolio management should be easy, although it's not uncommon for suppliers to charge more for their reporting suite.

As mentioned earlier, more and more suppliers are now moving to an architecture where the data being gathered by the project management package are stored in a relational database and reporting carried out using a BI tool. These tools are designed to be able to produce reports in both numerical or graphical format or a combination of both. The supplier will usually provide a set of prebuilt reports so you can either modify the existing ones or build new ones according to your need.

This is a very powerful facility. You could for instance produce reports which show your revenue and profitability by project over time, so you can look at the trend of what happens to your projects. If they all start profitable and somewhere say around testing they start to lose money then you can build an action plan to resolve this. You might want to show the loading of your team over time and by grouping. This would allow you to see that say your analyst or programming groups start to fall off a cliff into zero utilisation in a couple of months and that you'd better do something about this.

Reporting using BI tools is such a powerful feature that it will help you run your business. You can monitor the profitability of your entire project portfolio week-by-week or if you're an internal department track against budget, without even opening a spreadsheet. More than that, once senior management are used to seeing this level of reporting then lax processes lower down the food chain will become immediately apparent. This forces project managers to keep plans up to date and team members to fill timesheets in on time, which can only be good.

Collaboration features

Projects are essentially collaborative activities, where a project manager attempts to get the best out of a set of resources to deliver an end product.

More and more tools place an emphasis on collaboration, so as well as being able to share plans and documents, to provide discussion boards, instant messaging and facilities for review and comment on documents. One of the strengths of this is that discussions and review comments which usually end up in long e-mail or instant messaging trails are saved within the project management package in an orderly, accessible and searchable format. It also provides an audit trail that makes it easier to track decisions and settle any disputes you might have with suppliers or customers. If used properly, these can be excellent features, especially for a geographically dispersed team.

Training and user guides

Training will be important. I'd recommend you get your users trained by the supplier, so that people can ask questions. Usually this can be done remotely, rather than face-to-face, which keeps the costs down.

Most vendors will combine an on-boarding and training package and you'll have to pay a one-off charge for this. On-boarding isn't necessarily simple. You might have data to transfer from the package you're using now and most of these packages are highly configurable and they need to be set up appropriately for you. Also take a look at the user guides that come with the package. The best facilities tend to be searchable reference guides and short videos.

Pricing

Well the good news is that pricing starts at zero, but before you get too excited, you should note that vendors aren't charities. The strategy for many vendors is to start you off at low or no cost with a version of their software with limited functionality and then upsell when you inevitably start to find that you need to do more. Remember what we said earlier, once you start using one of these tools in anger, it becomes hard to move away. Suppliers know this. Going for the cheapest package before looking closely what it delivers is highly likely to be a waste of time and money.

The free or trial versions give you the opportunity to evaluate one or a number of packages to determine which is the right one for you. In an evaluation it's important you're clear about what you want to get from a package and try to attach priorities to your requirements. Make sure you don't try to evaluate too many packages, get down to a shortlist of three or four. When you decide which one best meets your requirements I'd strongly recommend you then try to use it with some real work. It's only then that you start to clearly identify any issues or omissions.

Pricing is often on a per-user basis, but sometimes charging is by active projects. You need to decide which model works for you. Be careful to ensure that any features that you've assumed are included for free really are included. It's common to charge extra for a BI package and for integrations with other software. Storage may be limited too. This can all result in the costs increasing dramatically above your initial assumptions so check what you're going to get for your money.

Key recommendations for buying a project management package

- Be clear what you want before you buy
- Check the browsers, devices and operating systems you use are supported by the package
- Is your data secure? Does the package support encryption of data in transit and at rest?
- Who owns your data? Make sure it's you and not the vendor
- Look for Gantt Charts, Kanban Boards, dependencies, constraints and multiple levels
- Don't chose a package that auto-schedules with no option to manually schedule tasks
- Producing reports should be easy. Packages with a relational database and a BI tool offer the most comprehensive and flexible reporting and analysis
- Make sure the package has timesheet capture for progress and financial tracking
- What integrations are supported? Integration with an accounting package or other collaboration tools may be important
- Does the tool allow you to manage portfolios of projects?
- How well does the tool allow you to manage resourcing at the project and portfolio level?
- How good are the training and user guides and what will start-up cost?
- What is the basis for charging, by user or project?

Shared workspaces

It's very difficult to make any project work without the ability to share documents. For a team who are geographically dispersed it's just about impossible

If you're going to collaborate effectively then you'll need to share workspaces to allow you to make the variety of materials produced and used by the project available to the whole team.

This can get a little complex. If you decide to go with the suite of office, collaboration and co-ordination tools available from bigger suppliers such as Google and Microsoft then most of this can be delivered in a reasonably integrated way from a single supplier. However by doing this you'll have to make compromises and it's unlikely you'll be sourcing the best of breed for each category of tool. In fact if one of the bigger suppliers manages to launch the best of breed package in every category then everyone else may as well pack up and go home, but usually this isn't the way things work.

If you are sourcing a variety of tools from different suppliers then you'll get some shared storage with each tool. Messaging tools will have their own space, so will project management tools and videoconferencing packages. Much of this will be transparent to you but what is essential is that each of the packages you choose interface with each other and in particular with your shared storage provider.

Storage

There are countless cloud storage vendors from the huge and impersonal giants to small enterprises offering a more personal and potentially cheaper service often using a chunk of someone else's server farm. Popular and well established vendors are Box, Dropbox, Google Drive, Microsoft OneDrive and Amazon Drive but you might want to look at smaller companies like Syncplicity, Tresorit and OwnCloud.

Pretty much all of these vendors will offer a facility where a local drive or file is synced to cloud storage. You can then modify either the cloud version or the local version and the changes will be reflected in both. However this can result in a 'last user wins' situation where if you change your local copy of a file, when it syncs with the shared version you may end up overwriting someone else's edits. This is more a document management system than true shared storage. The ideal in shared storage is where a shared document can be edited by several parties simultaneously and still maintain its integrity. This is true document sharing, often referred to as co-authoring and reflects the capabilities of the editing tools more than the storage provider. For instance the online versions of Microsoft's Office tools support co-authoring and so does Google's G-Suite. Microsoft and Google both allow you to co-author using Box and Dropbox as your file store as well as with OneDrive and Drive respectively. Neither Microsoft nor Google support co-authoring on each other's storage.

Security

Your storage is likely to contain commercially sensitive documents so you should be very concerned about its security. You should be looking for encryption both for data in transit and at rest. Most suppliers will provide this. You should also be concerned about how individuals gain access to the data. Ideally you'll have an SSO (Single Sign On) set up with the same security co-ordinated across all of the products in your collaboration and co-ordination suite. If you're not using SSO then you should look for vendors who offer multi-factor authentication and the ability to set a security policy e.g. forcing users to change passwords at a defined frequency and password composition rules.

Some of the smaller storage providers use security as their USP. For instance Tresorit promote themselves as 'the most secure cloud storage' and sync.com strongly promote their security credentials. Files are encrypted using a security key. Both Tresorit and sync.com provide zero-knowledge encryption which means they do not store a copy of this key. This means you and only you can decrypt your files. Both also offer two factor authentication and a host of other security options. Sync.com's servers are in Canada who have one of the most stringent privacy regimes in the world. Tresorit allows you to decide which country you'd like your data stored in so you can choose the jurisdiction that suits your needs best. If bulletproof security is vital to you then take a look at these providers.

Back-up and disaster recovery

If you don't want to run the risk of losing data, then you'll want your shared workspaces to be backed-up. So check what's included in the price. Is a weekly back-up sufficient for you? Some vendors will back-up on the fly, so any loss of data, accidental deletion etc. will be retrievable pretty much instantly. Can you specify your own back-up schedule and how easy and fast is it to retrieve old back-ups? Find out what your provider's back-up policy is and how flexible it is.

Be aware that the vast majority of data loss is caused by human error and while the back-ups carried out by your storage provider may cover that for a short period this will not be for ever. For instance deleted files on Google Drive and OneDrive go into their respective recycle bins. Google Drive automatically empties this bin after 30 days and OneDrive after 93 days. Once that has happened your file is gone for good. If this concerns you then you might want to look at a specialist back-up solution such as those offered by Backupify or Spinbackup.

You may also be interested in versioning. This allows you to access previous versions of a file, giving you an audit trail of what has been changed and the ability to correct an erroneous or unintended update with minimal fuss. Many suppliers provide document versioning.

Disaster recovery is also very important. How would your business be impacted if the facility where your files are stored flooded or suffered a fire and was out of action for a week or longer with no access to your data? You probably don't want to take such chances, so enquire about your vendor's disaster recovery processes. You should expect a back-up held off-site as a minimum and ideally that there is a hot standby facility so should the building where your files are held disappear into a hole in the ground, an instant switch is made to a geographically distant facility with minimal disruption. Instant switching is becoming more common given how easy it is to replicate servers over high speed data connections.

Multi-platform

Many storage providers work hand in glove with desktop based operating systems, so the cloud storage just appears as folders in a user's local storage. This is very slick and easy to use, but it may not necessarily work on every operating system in your network.

There's also no reason why your shared workspace shouldn't work with mobile devices. Some may advertise this as a feature. If this is important to you make sure that Android and iOS devices are supported.

Key recommendations in shared workspaces

- The simplest form of shared storage is where a local drive is synced to cloud storage. However this results in a 'last user wins' situation and is less shared storage than document management.
- The ideal is that one document can be edited by several parties simultaneously and maintain its integrity. This is known as co-authoring.
- Look for encryption in transit and at rest.
- Look for two-factor authentication to beat phishing and implement SSO.
- Versioning allows you to retrieve earlier versions of a document. It gives you an audit trail and a way of recovering from erroneous changes.
- Understand the vendor's back-up, versioning and disaster recovery procedures.
- Find out if the storage is accessible from all operating systems and mobile devices.

4

SECURITY

The biggest issue

Poor security can destroy the credibility of a remotely run team and it's important to understand that it's as much about how people act as it is the technology

Arguably security is the single biggest issue in remote working. When security comes to mind we tend to think about firewalls, encryption and secure connections but security is as much about the actions of the people on your team as it is about the technology.

In-house security teams concern themselves with all aspects of keeping a company's data and processes secure. This ranges from IT security, vetting of employees to the locks on the front and back doors.

Once the front door is opened and the operation spreads to potentially anywhere in the world then security risks are bound to increase.

Technology

While of course technology is the enabler for remote working, it's also a source of vulnerability. Remote employees could be using insecure Wi-Fi, computers with poor security or lose mobile devices containing sensitive information

Technology allows us to achieve stuff we'd never dreamed of even ten years ago and it is the principal enabler for remote working.

Remote working revives a whole lot of familiar challenges, many of which have already been fixed in the in-house working environment where removable storage is usually banned and Wi-Fi is encrypted and secure.

Remote resources could be working in cafes or other public areas with little or no security. They might lose mobile devices containing sensitive data. This all presents a much greater challenge for security officers than the comforting office environment does.

VPN and VDI

A Virtual Private Network (VPN) can be viewed as a secure encrypted pipe running on the public internet through which you can channel some or all data transmitted between one point e.g. a laptop computer and another, likely to be a server. VPN is readily available and relatively inexpensive. It means that wherever the employee uses their computer, laptop or mobile device as long as they access the cloud application via VPN their connection will be secure.

Signing up to a VPN provider or configuring your own VPN set up in-house is one of the best steps you can take to ensure security for remote workers and make certain that data will be far more secure in transit. It also allows you to build a secure link into your in-house applications, e-mail and secure servers. You can even provide some or all of the applications available on your in-house desktop to remote workers using VPN. However this is a two edged sword, while it provides a secure method of remote working, it also opens a back door into your network, so you need to ensure that users who log on to the VPN are fully authenticated. VPN also doesn't stop users downloading potentially sensitive data to their devices or uploading viruses from those devices to your network. To remedy these issues, you may wish to hide some parts of your network from remote access, protect the VPN with a firewall and ramp up your monitoring of miscreant activity.

Because of the way VPNs work they will inevitably slow things down but this isn't likely to be an issue other than for very high bandwidth applications like videoconferencing. The most important factors will be your proximity to the VPN server and the number of simultaneous users of that server. As with most things, you get what you pay for, the cheapest VPNs are likely to be the slowest. Before signing up for a VPN find out if you will take a performance hit from introducing it. There is no shortage of business VPN providers. Perimeter 81 Business, NordVPN Teams, Encrypt.me and VyprVPN are all good VPN providers right now.

The gold standard for secure remote access is to provide Virtual Desktop Infrastructure (VDI). This means that each desktop is running either in the cloud or on an in-house server sitting behind your firewall. The remote worker then connects to their desktop via the internet. No applications are run locally, no data is held locally and you can enforce virtually all of the security policies that you run in-house. VDI requires a lot of hardware centrally and has a high maintenance overhead so is relatively expensive, but if security is very important to you, this is the ideal set-up for remote working. VDI has been around for a long time with Citrix and VMWare two of the most established players in this market. Most of the big hosting providers e.g. Amazon AWS and Microsoft Azure will facilitate VDI in the cloud.

Even the best security will be hard pushed to completely stop employees or contractors from being able to download, e-mail or instant message files from your network or from shared storage to computers with poor security. If you want to try to close this gap there are a variety of tools like Teramind and Clearswift Adaptive DLP that can be used to identify and secure sensitive data in your network and monitor suspicious activity such as download or e-mailing of that data. Ideally highly sensitive data, such as customer information should never be open to access by remote workers, but in some circumstances e.g. remote call centres and customer service centres this is unavoidable. In these cases the software being used needs to be carefully designed to both keep data secure in transit and to limit the potential to be able to screenshot or photograph customer data.

Applications in the cloud

So while a VPN is secure, cloud application providers are also improving their act in terms of security. Encryption in transit and at rest isn't completely there yet but it's spreading fast and will soon be a hygiene factor for all business cloud applications where security is important. If employees are accessing communication and coordination software in the cloud then make sure the level of security provided by those applications is good. This is covered in detail in Chapter 3 - Technology.

If your application provider doesn't provide encrypted data in transit then you may want to consider using VPN access via a VPN service provider or an in house web server. It means that wherever the employee uses their computer, laptop or mobile device as long as they access the cloud application via VPN their connection will be secure. Data from the VPN service provider will go into the public internet once it gets past their server but each packet will be very difficult to attribute to an individual or company by any potential hacker at that end.

Sign on

Phishing is the easiest way for fraudsters to gain unauthorised access to applications and data. It is a form of fraud where the hacker masquerades as a reputable entity and tries to induce their target to reveal log on details, usually via a link embedded in the e-mail. You'll probably have received a few e-mails like this in your private e-mail box. Politicians have recently been the targets for this with phishing being used to harvest e-mails which are then leaked at election time.

However this is easily prevented with two-factor authentication. There are lots of different ways of achieving this from hardware token devices which require the user to enter a code to apps on mobile phones which produce a numerical or QR code to a simple text message via a mobile phone. Check your software supplier supports two-factor authentication. Ideally you should provide a Single Sign On (SSO) with two-factor authentication for your entire remote environment.

Many organisations find it a challenge to keep track of individuals working for them particularly where contract or temporary resource is concerned and where existing employees change roles. This becomes a lot more challenging when a large part of the workforce is remote, distributed around the world and likely to be on flexible contractual terms. Good Identity Management becomes important both to track who has access to what and to pick up when employees leave the company.

Information security

You'll probably be storing a whole lot of your valuable data in the cloud including plans, message history, chat boards, webcasts, recordings of meetings, training videos and project documentation. You may have a variety of different suppliers for this using different hosting providers. As mentioned earlier make sure each of these suppliers have adequate back-up and disaster recovery procedures and that contractually you're the owner of all of this data. If you use portable devices such as tablets and laptops it's prudent but expensive to supply every remote worker with an encrypted laptop to your company's standards. This guards against a security breach caused by someone leaving a laptop on a bus or train.

People

The single biggest security risk in any enterprise is the people who work for it.

You can have secure and encrypted messaging and videoconferencing but if an employee allows someone to read the messages or overhear a meeting then all of that encryption is useless.

Most videoconferencing and messaging applications allow guests to take part. In a previous role I used to attend a meeting with around 20 participants, internal and external to the company. In addition sometimes deputies turned up. It was often difficult to be sure that everyone at the meeting was supposed to be there. Adding to the confusion was the tendency for people to turn up late or leave before the end.

So be careful that everyone at your videoconference is permitted to be there. This is unlikely to be an issue if there are less than six of you but this can be a definite risk for larger meetings. If someone is trying to meeting-jump they're more likely to do it once the meeting is underway and everyone is distracted. There are options to help you block this. Most packages provide a waiting room facility where the meeting owner has to specifically admit each participant to the meeting and you can turn a sound on for when each participant joins. Some videoconferencing software also allows you to lock a meeting once it is underway. You might want to consider this for larger meetings where you're not familiar with all of the participants. It might also encourage people to arrive on time!!

Videoconferences and messaging should be password protected and you should never send out a link to a meeting which removes the need to enter ID and password. Many videoconferencing packages offer this facility for ease of use but don't use it, it offers carte blanche to someone who wants to sneak into your meeting.

There have been a number of incidents recently where a press photographer has managed to capture an image of a printed page of notes that a politician or one of their aides is carrying, revealing embarrassing detail about what they had been discussing behind closed doors. In a videoconference a high definition camera might well capture private or commercially sensitive information, so take care that the camera is capturing your face only!

The same goes for screen sharing, it's very easy to reveal something you didn't want to if you share the entire screen. Many videoconferencing applications give you the option of sharing an application or window rather than the entire screen. If not then close anything sensitive before you start the videoconference.

You also need to be aware if you're recording videoconferences that the recording could go anywhere once you've let a third party download it. This could be dangerous if say you revealed commercially sensitive information in the process of a sales call or were talking about something you wouldn't want to be made public. So don't record videoconferences as a matter of course, let all participants know when a meeting is being recorded and make sure you store the recordings securely where only authorised users can access them. If you are distributing recordings then be very careful that they do not contain anything that you wouldn't want to be made public.

Remote access security audits

Periodic audits provide an assurance that the right level of security is both in place and being maintained for remote working.

Given the security risks inherent in remote working, it makes sense to carrying out periodic audits of all aspects of your remote set up. This should cover not only the technology but also the rules in place and practices being followed by remote workers. This is sometimes referred to as Remote Access Penetration Testing and it is usual to ask independent security experts to carry this out.

This should cover:

- Hacking. The auditors attempt to find the ways through your remote IT security set up that a hacker would use to attack your systems and compromise your security. This would include probing IT systems for vulnerabilities as well as using techniques like phishing and fraudulent contact to test remote workers' security awareness.

- Remote worker security. The auditors would carry out hacking attacks on a sample of remote workers to test the security they have in place.

- Review of the remote IT security architecture and of the practices and training provided to remote workers to maintain security.

Key security recommendations

- Remote resources could be working in public areas with poor security and they might lose mobile devices containing sensitive data.
- Signing up to a VPN provider or configuring your own VPN set up is one of the best steps you can take to ensure security for remote workers.
- If security is paramount then look at using VDI (virtual desktops) but bear in mind that it's expensive to set up and maintain.
- If employees are accessing cloud applications then make sure the level of security provided by those applications is good.
- Chose cloud applications that support a security policy, two-factor authentication and preferably SSO.
- Be careful that everyone at a videoconference is permitted to be there.
- Make sure that sensitive information isn't accidentally screen-shared in a video conference
- Use monitoring and/or have policies that forbid remote employees from downloading data on to insecure local devices or printing sensitive data.
- Given the security risks inherent in remote working it makes sense to carry out regular Remote Security Audits.

5

LEGAL
FACTORS

Contractual

Cover all of your legal liabilities by publishing a home working policy

To ensure that you've covered all of your legal liabilities for home working, I'd strongly advise you publish a home working policy for employees and have this reviewed by a lawyer.

You'll need to consider:

- What you expect to provide to employees and what they are expected to provide e.g. computer, headset, high speed internet connection, furniture, heating and lighting etc.

- Who is responsible for insuring what equipment?

- If using their home as a base for work is allowed within the employee's rental/mortgage agreement

- If the risks associated with working from home are adequately covered within both employees and employers public liability insurance

- Expectations are set regarding remote employees attendance at meetings and with their managers either remotely, in the office or both

- Expectations are set regarding contact between employer and employee, so employees can't go off grid

- How performance will be monitored

- Do you want to have different contracts for home workers or at least ask them to sign home-working agreements?

- How IT and other support can be accessed and what hours it will be available

- Are there contractual issues or local rules that have to be addressed on working time?

- Security and computer abuse policy for home workers.

- Health and Safety requirements (see next section).

Health and Safety

In many jurisdictions Health and Safety is a legal responsibility of the employer. Make sure you assess the suitability of an employee's remote working environment

Depending on your local health and safety rules, when your own employees are working remotely you may need to assess the suitability of their working environment by carrying out a workplace risk assessment and making sure that your employer's liability insurance covers remote working.

You should also consider offering advice to employees about looking after their own health while working at home. Spending long hours hunched over a laptop or a mobile device is unlikely to be good for posture and back health. Some employers provide a workstation and chair to remote workers to avoid being subject to a legal case from an employee who has sustained an injury from working remotely.

While most employees seem to enjoy the benefits of flexibility and the reduction or removal of the daily commute, there can be negative effects on mental health. Increased stress can arise from 24/7 working. It can affect family life, may increase the intensity of work and blur of the boundaries between paid work and personal life. Again, it's worth considering providing advice to home working employees regarding potential impacts on their mental health and putting in place an independent counselling service through an Employee Assistance Program (EAP).

Discrimination

Are remote employees being treated in a sufficiently different way to their office based equivalents that this could be viewed as discrimination?

Are remote employees being treated more like workhorses than their office equivalents? In some industries a disproportionate number of remote workers are female. Practice that appears to favour office based employees against remote workers by hours worked, lack of consideration for promotions and involvement in the company, while being bad practice could also lead to accusations of discrimination.

You may want to consider educating managers to rule out his sort of bad practice.

Bullying and Harassment

Bullying and harassment become more difficult to detect in a remote environment, but have a corrosive effect on morale and can lead to legal action

Bullying can be an issue in an office environment, but it's a lot harder to pick up when it transforms into cyber bullying in a remote team. Cyber bullying could consist of unkind emails, frequent interruptions during videoconference meetings and overly aggressive emails or messages from managers. From the comfort and safety of their home it's easier for employees to lose inhibition and exhibit hurtful or bullying behaviour, particularly where social and work events merge in the remote social events proposed in Chapter 2 – How to Build Successful Remote Teams. With employees physically isolated from each other, doubt and insecurities may creep in and the actions of other employees, and particularly managers might be more readily misinterpreted.

Employers need to be attuned to this. I'd recommend that existing policies are reviewed and where appropriate modified to cover cyber bullying. Employees should be notified both of the courses of action open to them should they feel they are victims of bullying and of the standards they are expected to uphold in a remote working environment. Disciplinary action, if required, is likely to be a lot more straightforward in a remote environment given most interactions between employees are electronic and so highly likely to be available as evidence in a complaint or dispute.

Employers should also give thought to proactive monitoring and training to avoid incidents arising. Bullying and harassment as well as leaving companies open to legal action, have a corrosive effect on team spirit and productivity and may lead to the loss of valued employees.

Confidential Information

Beware of confidential client data ending up being printed out and used as scrap paper

Beware of the legal implications of sensitive data ending up on remote workers' computers or being printed and ending up in non-confidential waste or maybe even the remote worker's children's classroom as scrap paper!! You need policies in place to reduce the risk of this happening.

6
CONCLUSION

People

You're going to need significantly different skills to those used to manage local teams to be successful as a remote project manager

Remote project management is here to stay and is set to grow exponentially. Working remotely truly is the future of work and the COVID-19 epidemic has accelerated its arrival. Employees like the notion of ditching the daily commute and all of the indications are that as a result they're more productive. Employers win as well. They save money on office space and can source talented people from all over the world without having to worry about fighting through red tape to get work visas approved and cover the expense of relocation costs. Most companies are also interested in boosting their environmental credentials and remote working hits a lot of targets for this too.

COVID-19 also emphasised the value of remote working in disaster preparedness and recovery. Many companies were able to carry out a relatively smooth transition from office to home working that would not have been possible without an existing remote working infrastructure.

Global enterprises have been working in a distributed way for many years, setting up service centres and back office facilities worldwide and this trend will only grow as these companies look to both drive down costs and be 'local' companies worldwide.

Setting up a team for remote work isn't quite as simple as buying everyone a headset, camera and copy of Skype. You're going to need significantly different skills to successfully manage remote teams to those needed to manage local teams. Project managers, in fact all types of manager need to appreciate this and make changes to the way they work.

Managing people who may not be able see your face and are from different traditions and cultures can be a real challenge. To do this and meet the tough deadlines that are the norm in running projects is even more difficult.

Building team spirit is going to be a lot harder and you need to take care that you don't impose your cultural norms on people who come from very different backgrounds to you. Credibility is that much harder to gain and a lot easier to lose.

This isn't just about making a tweaks to how you manage teams now. Be prepared to work harder and more flexibly than you would with an office based team. You're going to need to demonstrate that the disembodied voice they hear in teleconferences is in control and knows their stuff. You may find the line between work and personal life starts to blur if you find yourself working with people in other time zones.

Having said all of that, you'll be acquiring a much sought after skill and one that's going to be in more and more demand. You'll also have the opportunity to work with people from different backgrounds and cultures and to be challenged by ideas that may not have ever occurred to you. This will be a stimulating environment to work in and one that accelerates your growth and learning. I've certainly found that.

Technology

The technology is already there and improving rapidly. Knowledge is becoming the world's most valuable resource and governments are under pressure to build the infrastructure to support its marketing.

The technology is already there to support remote project management and is improving at a fast pace in what is a very competitive marketplace. You only have to look at the speed that vendors are launching products in the collaboration and co-ordination tools market to see that this is a sector experiencing high growth rates.

Having said that, in such a crowded marketplace it can be hard to decide which way to go and which tools are best of breed. The good news is that with the level of competition both hardware and software are improving at a very rapid rate and pricing is being put under pressure.

The single biggest advance in technology will come, as for many sectors, from Artificial Intelligence where there is the promise of a huge improvement in language translation technology. This should remove the biggest barrier to a global team working well together. At the moment, while acknowledging that other languages are available, this tends to depend on the quality of English spoken by all participants but better and faster language translation software will remove this as an issue.

The speed and quality of communication links is also an issue worldwide. Some regions have much better links than others, but this is an issue that will gradually diminish with increased bandwidth and superfast internet speeds becoming the norm. The roll out of

5G cellular networks worldwide is likely to be a major factor in rapidly increasing access to fast internet connections. 5G bypasses the need to upgrade aging telephony infrastructure or dig holes and install new cabling. The ideal end game is a video conference where all participants can both see and hear each other clearly.

The more global project teams become, the greater the pressure will be on country governments to rapidly increase the roll out of fast internet infrastructure to remain competitive in the marketing of what increasingly is becoming the world's single most valuable resource, knowledge.

Glossary

5G – is the new generation of cellular network infrastructure (superseding 4G) and is capable of theoretical speeds of up to 10 gigabits per second.

Active Listening – is a technique that is often used in counselling, training, and solving disputes. It requires the listener to concentrate, understand, respond and then remember what is being said.

Agile – group of software development methods that promote the development of solutions through collaboration between self-organising, cross-functional teams.

Artificial Intelligence – computer systems able to perform tasks that currently require human intelligence, for example visual perception, speech recognition, decision-making, and translation between languages.

Body Language – is a type of non-verbal communication where physical behaviors, as opposed to words, are used to convey information.

Business Intelligence (BI) Tool - this is a tool which prepares and presents data in a form which helps decision makers to make more effective data-driven decisions.

Chat Board – is an online discussion area where people with similar interests discuss topics. The contents of these discussions are usually available to be searched.

Collaboration and Coordination Software – one or a number of software packages that facilitate remote teams collaborating, communicating and sharing information, together with software that allows a project manager to control and coordinate that team.

Collaboration software – Collaborative software or groupware is application software designed to help people involved in a common task to achieve their goals.

Content Sharing – refers to sharing the contents of an individual window or the whole screen in a videoconferencing package.

Gantt Chart – a representation of a project plan in a bar chart, as promoted by Henry Gantt in the early 20th century.

Hosted Service – where a supplier of an application hosts that application on their own servers and charges typically by use.

Instant Messaging – is the exchange of near real-time messages through a software application.

Kanban Boards - is an agile tool used to help visualize work. Kanban boards use cards, columns and continuous improvement to help Agile teams commit to work, and get it done.

Nonviolent communication (NVC) - is a way of removing the negative and adversarial elements from conversation to achieve a better result.

On-premise – software is installed and runs on computers on the premises of the organisation using the software, rather than in the cloud.

Organisation Chart – (often called an org chart) is a diagram that shows the structure of an organisation and the relationships and relative ranks of the people shown in that chart.

Project Management Software – an application typically delivered as a service over the internet which facilitates the management of geographically dispersed teams.

Project Plan – visual aid showing the tasks and resources required to complete a project, typically a plan is represented as a Gantt chart and produced using Project Management Software.

QR Code – Quick Response Code is a type of two-dimensional barcode initially developed for use by the Japanese car industry. They are now used much more widely and in a similar way to standard bar codes to identify properties of the item they are attached to or associated with.

SSO (Single Sign On) – allows a user to log on to multiple independent software systems with a single username and password.

Town Hall – a meeting where all of a company's staff are brought together, sometimes referred to as an 'all-staff meeting'.

Two-Factor Authentication – an additional level of security where a user is asked to provide a second level of validation after they've entered their username and password. This varies from being asked to quote a memorable phrase or word to keying a code produced by a hardware device.

VDI – Virtual desktop infrastructure (VDI) is virtualisation technology that hosts a desktop operating system on a centralised server in a data centre

Videoconferencing – is a technology that allows users in different locations to hold face-to-face meetings without having to physically move to a single location.

VPN – A Virtual Private Network can be viewed as a secure encrypted pipe running on the public internet through which you can channel some or all data transmitted between one point e.g. a laptop computer and another (likely to be a server)

Wall of Fame – a set of images of people on a team, together with information about themselves such as interests and hobbies.

Waterfall – method of project delivery where each stage 'flows' into the next, usually comprising requirements, design, build and test stages.

Webinar – a seminar that takes place over the internet, typically using either specific Webinar software or a videoconferencing package.

Index

Credits/Notes

[1] Flexible: friend or foe? – by Vodafone 8 Feb 2016

[2] Dell *really* wants you to work from home ... if you want - by Jeanne Sahad CNN Money June 9 2016

[3,5] The Psychology of Interpersonal Behaviour – Michael Argyle

[4] When Italians Chat, Hands and Fingers Do the Talking - Rachel Donadio – New York Times June 30, 2013

[6] Nonviolent Communication - Marshall B. Rosenberg, Ph D.

[7] The Difference: How the Power of Diversity Creates Better Groups, Firms, Schools, and Societies by Scott E. Page

[8] Want to understand accented speakers better? Practice, practice, practice. Melissa Michaud Baese-Berk, Associate Professor of Linguistics, University of Oregon The Conversation April 3, 2019

[9] Sapiens A Brief History of Humankind – Yuval Nosh Harari - Vintage 2011

[10] Epson EcoTank survey - One can be the loneliest number — many UK freelancers feel lonely and isolated following leap to self-employment. Epsom 4-9-2018

[11] Body Language; Around the World - Nuria Nakajima 30 March 2016 LinkedIn Pulse

[12] Cultural Context Inventory - Claire B. Halverson (1993)

[13] Effective Multicultural Teams: Theory and Practice (Advances in Group Decision and Negotiation) Halverson and Tirmizi   22 Jun 2008

[14] Sit less and move more to reduce risk of early death, study says. Nicola Davis - The Guardian Health 14 Jan 2019

[15] The Definitive Book of Body Language - Barbara and Allan Pease 1978

[16] The reason Zoom calls drain your energy By Manyu Jiang 22nd April 2020 BBC Remote Control

[17] Quiet The Mind – Matthew Johnstone - Robinson 5th April 2012

[18] Working anytime, anywhere - The effects on the world of work International Labour Organisation and the European Foundation for the improvement of Living and Working Conditions – 2017

An acknowledged expert in project management, Gren Gale has dedicated his working life to managing projects of all sizes effectively and efficiently.

Over the last 15 years he has successfully managed projects across all five continents and gained an unrivalled expertise in what it takes to make running a project remotely work.

Founder and CEO of PM Results, a company set up to enable businesses to implement world class project management practices, he is a Prince 2 practitioner and professional Scrum Master.

For more information visit **PMresults.co.uk**